MicroSets

Putting Economic Theory To Work

PATRICK O'DONOGHUE

AND

TANYA ROBERTS

WITH

MARY EYSENBACH AND JOHN FLOYD

W · W · NORTON & COMPANY

NEW YORK · LONDON

First Edition

W. W. Norton & Company, Inc. 500 Fifth Avenue, New York, N.Y. 10036
W. W. Norton & Company, Ltd. 25 New Street Square, London EC4A 3NT

Library of Congress Cataloging in Publication Data

O'Donoghue, Patrick.
   Microsets: Putting Economic Theory to Work

   Includes index.
   1. Microeconomics.   I. Roberts, Tanya, joint
author.   II. Title.
HB171.5.044   1981   338.5   80-14263
ISBN 0-393-95141-3

---

1 2 3 4 5 6 7 8 9 0

CONTENTS

PREFACE

This book is a textbook, but of a different type. It is designed to complement, not replace, the didactic textbook. Its keynote is the systematic application of economic concepts to specific problems and issues.

This text is based on three premises. First, one of the most effective ways to teach microeconomics is to apply its concepts in a wide range of settings. Second, as useful as certain specific concepts are, even more valuable is the overall analytical approach of microeconomics. Third, a focus on specific problems and issues compels an emphasis on those microeconomic principles which have substantial analytical power.

The theme of this book is both the power and utility of microeconomics. On the one hand, the book seeks to arouse student interest by demonstrating the power and thus the utility of microeconomic concepts. On the other hand, it strives to teach students how to apply microeconomic principles, both so that they might learn them and so that they might later use them to their benefit.

The fourteen chapters of this text are grouped into five sections, with a concise overview introducing each section. The chapters follow a common pattern. A situation—actual or imaginary, but with realistic implications—is presented. Questions are posed about the situation, and responses are developed. The book thus employs the Socratic method or the question/discussion format to teach microeconomics. To further enhance this approach, the economic concepts central to each chapter are identified at the beginning of the chapter.

The scope of this text is broad, which illustrates how wide the range of microeconomics has become. Although self-contained, this book is intended to be utilized in conjunction with a didactic textbook. Students may, therefore, often wish to refer to the latter for additional discussion of specific concepts used in this book.

This text is primarily designed for students taking a solid course in intermediate microeconomics. It may also be suitable for more advanced courses at the introductory level. Further, because of its emphasis on analyzing problems and issues, the book may prove useful to advanced students. An understanding of mathematics beyond basic algebra and geometry is not required.

Two emphases are maintained throughout the book. One is understanding the mechanisms underlying economic concepts. The other is pursuing the general implications of the specific cases discussed. The first emphasis reflects our experience that it is not too valuable to understand economic concepts only in mechanical terms. Rather, these concepts become much more powerful tools when they are understood in what is often called intuitive terms. The second emphasis is inherent in our approach since the teaching power of specific cases is largely dissipated if the implications beyond the case are not developed.

The forerunner of this text was a series of problem sets used at the University of Washington. Those problem sets were written by us and by our two coauthors—Mary Eysenbach now at Knox College and John Floyd currently at the University of Toronto. The solid work of both these economists played an important part in the development of this book.

Students at the University of Washington offered suggestions about the original problem sets and thus contributed to this text. The book has also benefited from the discerning comments of other economists, who read the manuscript in whole or in part, including Elizabeth Clayton of the University of Missouri-St. Louis, Bernard Saffran of Swarthmore College, Lowell Bassett of the University of Washington, Peter Temin of the Massachusetts Institute of Technology, and Paul Malatesta of Colgate University.

During the last several months Tonie Gatch has played a critical and wide-ranging role in the production of the final manuscript. Early in the book's history the versatile work of Jacqueline Reis was invaluable. Midway in its course the text benefited from the thoughtful editing of Melissa Culverwell and from the careful typing of Priscilla DeWolf. The final figures and tables were expertly prepared by Erin O'Donoghue. Still others contributed at different times to the manuscript's progress, including Mary Olson, Elizabeth Sayre, David DeWolf, and Kara Spitler.

Don Lamm of Norton has been a pivotal figure in the development of this text. His specific suggestions have been excellent, but most significant, he persistently encouraged us to complete this book, even when such appeared difficult because of other commitments.

We gratefully acknowledge the contributions of those noted above. Without question the book has benefited from their efforts. Even so, we as the primary authors remain responsible for its contents.

Patrick O'Donoghue, Ph.D., M.D.
Tanya Roberts, Ph.D.

Denver, Colorado
Washington, D.C.

November 1979

MicroSets

Putting Economic Theory to Work

I

FUNDAMENTAL ECONOMIC PRINCIPLES

The subject of Section I is the traditional core of microeconomic theory. The principles emphasized here have been used in most instances for many years. A thorough understanding of these principles is critical to learning how to apply economic concepts to policy issues. Often, important insights can be derived through the use of these principles alone. Further, they constitute the cornerstone for other types of economic theory used even more frequently to analyze policy questions.

A favorite subject of economists is the simple world of shipwrecked Robinson Crusoe and his man Friday. The simplicity of their nonindustrial, otherwise uninhabited island spotlights the basics of decision making. Chapter 1 continues this tradition, albeit with the substitution of Robyn Christian for Friday. The chapter highlights the gains that can be realized through cooperation and specialization, but points out that to attain these gains agreement must be reached on the distribution of income, often a thorny issue. Discrimination is common in human societies, and the chapter analyzes its impact in the island setting. The chapter also considers whether Robinson and Robyn can gain by trading in a nearby market.

Demand and supply analysis is an ancient craft among economists. While overused at times, its potency remains strong. Chapter 2 illustrates the use of demand and supply theory by analyzing the impact of different events on a set of integrated markets. The chapter's setting is the American orange industry with its three producing centers of California, Texas, and Florida. The chapter starts with demand and supply curves, and then looks in both directions. It looks inward to comprehend the forces leading to market equilibrium and to understand the factors responsible for demand and supply elasticity. It looks outward to assess the effects of different shocks on the orange markets. For example, it analyzes the impact of an increase in western freight rates on orange prices in California, Florida, and New York.

The focus of Chapter 3 is marginality—a cornerstone of consumer and producer decision making. Four cases are employed to illustrate different aspects of this concept. One is a New York travel agency debating the addition of a new tour. Another is a Massachusetts student deciding how to allocate her study time; the third is a Georgian observing road-building practices in India. The fourth and most complex centers on a Michigan welfare agency considering two alternative programs. Under one program eligible families will receive an unrestricted cash payment, while under the other they will receive a rent subsidy. These programs are illustrative of the two major approaches that have been used to reduce poverty in this country—the cash subsidy approach and the income-in-kind approach.

Chapter 4 shows an entrepreneur at work, in this case Dmitri Filippov of the Poltava Bakery. In so doing it illustrates the dynamics of profit maximization at the firm level. The Poltava produces two outputs; it uses several variable inputs but has one fixed input. The bakery's production function therefore reflects the law of diminishing returns. The so-called "invisible hand" is prominent in this chapter, as market prices perform the critical but hidden function of informing producers and consumers that changes have occurred. The chapter also considers work satisfaction and implicit costs, and assesses the impact that these factors have on production and employment decisions.

Chapter 5 discusses the time-honored model of perfect competition, which forms the baseline for many types of economic analysis. The setting is the taxicab industry in the hypothetical Texas city of San Cristobal. The chapter carefully considers the conditions necessary for perfect competition. It examines the perfectly competitive industry both from a firm standpoint and from an industry perspective. That is, the chapter both analyzes the actions of individual firms and derives the long-run equilibrium position of the industry as a whole. Another important concept is also discussed—the net benefit of an industry to a community.

Important Concepts

Production
Consumption
Scarcity
Economic Problem
Specialization
Comparative Advantage
Distribution of Income
Discrimination
Gains from Trade
Gains from Cooperation
Losses from Discrimination
Negotiation
Production Possibility Frontier
Consumption Line
Terms of Trade

1
Castaways
on Their Island
A Look at
Basic Economic Problems

A multitude of coconut trees crowns the island on which Robinson
Crusoe finds himself. An abundance of fish swims in its neighboring
waters. Having already attended to his shelter and clothing needs,
Robinson's primary concern is to obtain sufficient food. He can harvest
coconuts at the rate of 1 coconut per four hours of effort. Analogously,
he can catch fish at the rate of 1 fish per four hours of effort.

1. Does Robinson have an economic problem?

2. At the other end of the island is another castaway, Robyn Christian,
who is a better climber than Robinson, but a poorer fisher. She can pick
coconuts at the rate of 1 coconut per two hours of effort, while eight
hours of effort are required for her to catch 1 fish. Both Robyn and
Robinson work 40 hours each week either picking coconuts or catching
fish.
  Draw in Figure 1−1 the line representing the maximum combinations
of fish and coconuts that Robinson can obtain by working 40 hours per
week. This line is termed his production possibility frontier. Carry out
the same procedure for Robyn in Figure 1−2. As an example illustrating
how to construct these frontiers, one point on Robinson's frontier will be
the number of fish and the number of coconuts that he secures when he
devotes all his time to fishing.

3. Both Robinson and Robyn prefer to eat the same number of fish
and coconuts. Given these tastes, how many fish and coconuts will each
produce and consume?
  To determine the answer graphically, plot in Figures 1−1 and 1−2
consumption lines which represent the one-to-one consumption preference. In each figure the intersection of this line with the production

5

Figure 1-1

Production/Consumption by Robinson

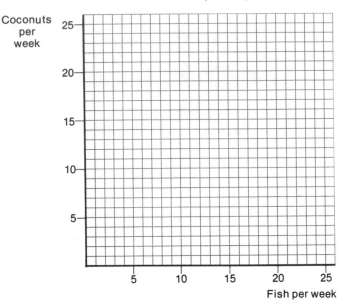

Figure 1-2

Production/Consumption by Robyn

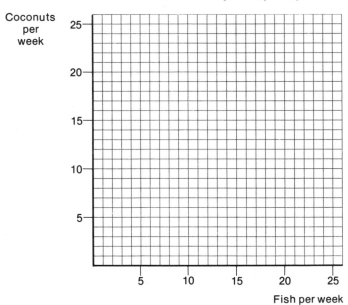

possibility frontier is the production/consumption point of the respective person.

4. Upon exploration Robyn and Robinson discover each other. After some interchange, the two agree to pool their weekly production of fish and coconuts. Each also agrees to work 40 hours per week.

In this cooperative setting which of the two should catch most of the fish because he or she is more adept at fishing? Which should pick most of the coconuts because of superior ability in that activity?

5. Keeping in mind the response to the previous question, draw in Figure 1−3 the combined production possibility frontier of Robinson

Figure 1-3

Combined Production/Consumption

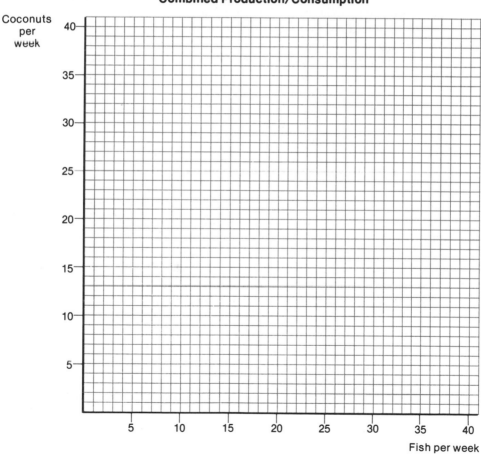

and Robyn. Also plot in this figure the consumption line representing their preference to consume the same number of fish and coconuts.

In the cooperative setting how many fish and coconuts will the two individuals jointly produce and consume? How many fish and coconuts will each produce? Is their combined production/consumption now larger or smaller than it was before?

6. In the cooperative setting how many fish and coconuts will Robyn consume? How many will Robinson consume? Assume that neither individual wishes to consume fractional fish or coconuts.

7. While they had not met prior to their island experience, both Robinson and Robyn were raised in societies which prescribed distinctly different roles for women and men. In general, the social codes in their earlier environments called for men to earn the livelihood for the family and for women to maintain the household and raise the children. If the restrictions placed on women by these codes were transposed to this island setting, Robyn would not be able to work as efficiently either fishing or harvesting coconuts. Her fishing productivity would decline to 1 fish per 12 hours of effort, and her proficiency picking coconuts would fall to 1 coconut per 4 hours of effort.

If Robinson and Robyn decide to conform to the social customs of their previous environments, what will be the impact on their combined production of fish and coconuts? The two individuals will continue to work cooperatively; each still prefers to consume an equal number of fish and coconuts; and each will work 40 hours per week.

8. After several months Robyn and Robinson discover a village on a neighboring island. Fish and coconuts can be readily traded in the marketplace of this village at the prevailing rate of 1 coconut for 1 fish. While trips to the neighboring island require effort, they are also pleasurable. As a result, neither Robinson nor Robyn includes trip time in the work week of 40 hours. Robyn and Robinson decided not to adopt the social codes of their earlier environments, and thus the restrictions on Robyn described in the previous question do not apply here. If they choose to do so, both individuals can travel to the nearby market sufficiently often that spoilage losses are insignificant. Robyn still prefers to consume an equal number of fish and coconuts as does Robinson.

If Robinson and Robyn do not cooperate, how many fish and coconuts will the latter produce? How many will she consume? How many fish and coconuts will Robinson produce? How many will he consume? Can Robinson and Robyn increase their combined production by cooperating?

DISCUSSION

1. To pose an economic problem, a situation must entail the necessity to allocate scarce resources among alternative ends. Such a necessity characterizes this situation. Robinson's time is scarce, i.e., limited to twenty-four hours per day. He must allocate this time among three alternative activities: picking coconuts, catching fish, and leisure. He therefore has an economic problem.

2. If Robinson devotes all his work time to harvesting coconuts, he will pick 10 per week. Similarly, if he spends all his time fishing, he will catch 10 fish per week. Both of these points are on Robinson's production possibility frontier. In Figure 1−4 point *A* represents his situation when he is only harvesting coconuts, and point *B* when he is only fishing. His production possibility frontier is a straight line between these points. That is, all maximum combinations of fish and coconuts that Robinson can obtain by working 40 hours per week lie on this line. For example, if Robinson spends 60 percent of his work time harvesting coconuts and the other 40 percent catching fish, he will secure 6 of the former and 4 of the latter.

Figure 1-4

Production/Consumption by Robinson

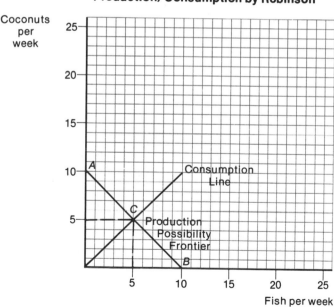

Robyn's production possibility frontier is constructed in the same way as Robinson's. It is depicted in Figure 1–5. If Robyn spends all her work time harvesting coconuts, she will obtain 20 per week; if she devotes all her time to fishing, she will catch 5 per week. The former situation is represented by point *A* in Figure 1–5, and the latter by point *B*. As in Robinson's case, Robyn's production possibility frontier is the straight line between these points.

Figure 1-5

Production/Consumption by Robyn

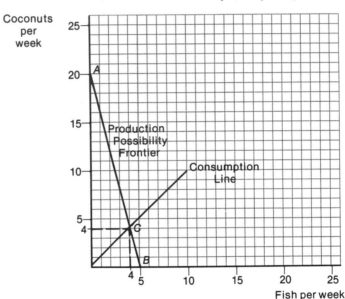

3. The line representing Robinson's one-to-one consumption preference is shown in Figure 1–4. It intersects Robinson's production possibility frontier at point *C* where he produces and consumes 5 coconuts and 5 fish per week. The one-to-one consumption line for Robyn is displayed in Figure 1–5. It intersects her production possibility frontier at point *C* where she consumes 4 units of each commodity.

Thus, while Robinson and Robyn have the same tastes, their differing skills lead to different weekly production/consumption. In this instance Robinson is better off because his equal ability to obtain coconuts or fish is more consonant with the one-to-one consumption preference than are Robyn's unequal skills. However, this need not be so. For example, if both Robinson and Robyn prefer to consume 4 coconuts per 1 fish,

10

Robinson's production/consumption would be 8 coconuts and 2 fish, while Robyn's would be 10 coconuts and 2½ fish.

4. Robinson is more adept at catching fish than is Robyn, while the reverse holds for harvesting coconuts. Robinson thus has a comparative advantage in catching fish, and Robyn has a comparative advantage in picking coconuts. Robinson should therefore catch most of the fish and Robyn should pick most of the coconuts.

5. The same general approach is used to construct the combined production possibility frontier as was employed to determine the individual frontiers. If both individuals devote all their time to coconut harvesting, their joint output will be 30 per week (i.e., 20 coconuts picked by Robyn and 10 by Robinson). Conversely, if they spend all their time fishing, their combined output will be 15 fish (i.e., 5 fish caught by Robyn and 10 by Robinson). These points are depicted respectively as points *A* and *C* in Figure 1–6. Robyn and Robinson can attain all the production possibilities on a straight line between these points. To do so they should divide their time equiproportionally between the two activities. That is, if Robyn spends two-thirds of her time fishing and one-third harvesting coconuts, Robinson should divide his time in the same way.

However, Robinson and Robyn can attain greater outputs by taking advantage of their comparative skills. To illustrate this point, assume that they start by devoting all their time to harvesting coconuts. They now decide that they want to increase their production of fish. Who should do the fishing? The answer is Robinson because he is the more skilled at this activity. Thus, as the two individuals progressively shift from exclusive coconut production to production of both fish and coconuts, Robinson should increasingly devote his time to fishing, with Robyn continuing to spend all her time harvesting coconuts.

They should continue in this way until Robinson spends all his time fishing and Robyn all her time harvesting coconuts. At that point their combined output will be 10 fish and 20 coconuts, i.e., point *B* in Figure 1–6. If after reaching point *B* Robyn and Robinson desire to further increase their output of fish, their only alternative is for Robyn to shift progressively from coconut production to fish production.

The combined production possibility frontier is thus two contiguous straight lines. One links points *A* and *B*; the other links points *B* and *C*. This frontier is depicted in Figure 1–6. The line representing the one-to-one consumption preference is also displayed in this figure. It is constructed in the same way as before.

As indicated in Figure 1–6, the combined production possibility frontier intersects the one-to-one consumption line at point *D* where

Figure 1-6

Combined Production/Consumption

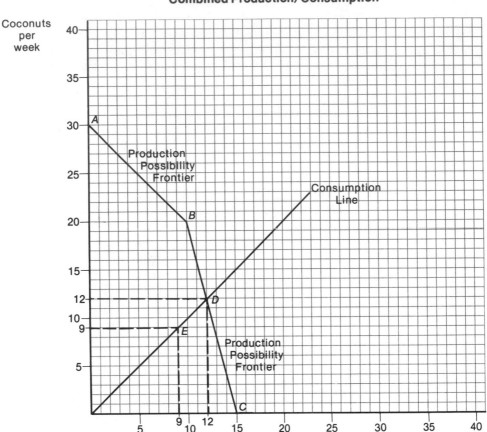

Robinson and Robyn produce and consume 12 coconuts and 12 fish per week. To attain this joint production, Robinson devotes all his time to fishing and catches 10 fish; Robyn obtains 2 fish and 12 coconuts by spending 16 hours fishing and 24 hours harvesting coconuts.

As noted, their combined production/consumption in the cooperative setting is 12 coconuts and 12 fish per week. In contrast, when Robyn and Robinson operated independently, their combined production/consumption was 9 units of each commodity (i.e., point *E* in Figure 1–6). The two individuals have thus markedly increased their production/consumption by cooperating. They achieve this result because cooperation enables them to specialize and to thereby take advantage of their differing skills.

If their skills were similar, there would be no such gain from cooperation. In this instance, specialization would confer no strong advantage. This illustrates the general point that cooperation and specialization will be most beneficial in those instances when the skills of those involved are both different and complementary, as is true in this case.

6. An argument can be made that Robinson would enter the cooperative arrangement as long as he was not worse off than before. Far more likely however, he will not conclude the agreement unless he is better off than before. The same reasoning applies to Robyn. In the independent setting Robinson produced and consumed 5 coconuts and 5 fish, while the corresponding figures for Robyn are 4 units of each commodity. Since their combined production in the cooperative setting is 12 coconuts and 12 fish, Robinson must consume fewer than 8 coconuts and 8 fish because Robyn's consumption must exceed the 4 coconuts and 4 fish that she consumed previously. By similar logic, Robyn must now consume fewer than 7 coconuts and 7 fish.

Because of the one-to-one consumption preference Robyn must consume an equal number of fish and coconuts. The same is true for Robinson. If bargaining between the two individuals temporarily produced an allocation of the two commodities which violated the one-to-one consumption preference, the allocation would be unstable since each person could better his or her position through further trade. For example, if Robyn had 7 coconuts and 5 fish and if Robinson had 5 coconuts and 7 fish, 2 coconuts would be worthless to Robyn, while 2 fish would be valueless to Robinson. An incentive thus exists for Robyn to trade 1 coconut for 1 fish and for Robinson to make the reverse trade. At the conclusion of this trade the commodity allocation is stable since Robyn has the same number of fish and coconuts as Robinson.

Since each individual must be better off than before, since each must consume an equal number of fish and coconuts, and since neither will consume fractional units, only two possible consumption patterns exist. Robinson and Robyn can each consume 6 coconuts and 6 fish. Alternatively, Robinson can consume 7 units of each product, with Robyn consuming the other 5. Which of these two consumption patterns will prevail depends on the negotiating abilities of the two individuals. If Robyn is the superior negotiator, the former pattern will result; conversely, if Robinson is more adept, the latter pattern will prevail.

This question illustrates two important points. First, negotiation is an important method of resolving disputes in a small group, such as the two-person group discussed here. When the range of possible outcomes is small as is true in this case, negotiation usually produces an agreement. As this range widens, negotiation becomes progressively more difficult, although the potential gains from negotiation increase.

Second, inherent in cooperation and specialization is the distribution of income issue. That is, it is necessary for the involved parties to agree on how to divide the joint output. In many instances, including the case discussed here, resolution of the distribution issue is likely because the gains from cooperation and specialization are large. In general, the larger such gains, the easier it will be to satisfy all involved individuals. Even so, many cooperative ventures, including profitable ones, have collapsed because of failure to reach agreement on the distribution of income.

7. Robinson should continue to spend his entire work week fishing. He will therefore catch 10 fish per week. As a result of the restrictions placed on Robyn, she must now devote all her work time to coconut production in order to match Robinson's weekly output of 10 fish. Their combined weekly output is thus now 10 fish and 10 coconuts as compared to their previous production of 12 units of each commodity. Accepting the social codes of their past environments therefore costs Robinson and Robyn 2 fish and 2 coconuts per week.

The restrictions on women discussed here constitute discrimination based on sex. Unlike racial discrimination, sexual discrimination is often stated in positive rather than negative terms. For example, women should not drive taxicabs, repair telephone lines, or fish in deep waters because these pursuits are too dangerous for women. While these and similar restrictions may protect women to some extent, they also limit the options available to women and reduce their work efficiency, as is true here for Robyn.

In this case the acceptance of discriminatory social codes reduces total output. This result holds generally. That is, a trade-off exists between discrimination and the production of goods and services. In general, the more stringent the discriminatory practices, the lower will be total output. A society may be happier practicing rigid sexual discrimination, but it must pay the price of having less output. Illustrating this point, Robinson and Robyn may feel more comfortable complying with the discriminatory practices that they were previously taught, but in doing so they will have fewer coconuts and fewer fish.

8. Since coconuts and fish can be readily traded in the nearby market at the rate of 1 fish for 1 coconut, Robyn will devote her entire work effort to the activity in which she has a comparative advantage, i.e., harvesting coconuts. Her weekly production will thus be 20 coconuts and 0 fish. She will take 10 coconuts to the market and will trade them for 10 fish. Her weekly consumption will therefore be 10 units of each commodity.

While Robinson can trade in the nearby market, he gains no advantage by doing so. In the market the terms of trade are 1 coconut for 1 fish. This means that the price of 1 fish is 1 coconut, and conversely, that the price of 1 coconut is 1 fish. Unlike Robyn, the cost to Robinson of producing one more coconut is one less fish. Similarly, his cost of producing another fish is the loss of a coconut. That being the case, no gains from trade flow to Robinson. He is equally well off producing 10 coconuts and trading 5 coconuts for 5 fish, or producing 10 fish and trading 5 fish for 5 coconuts, or producing 5 units of each commodity and making no trades. In any event his weekly consumption will be 5 coconuts and 5 fish.

There is now no incentive to cooperate since the two individuals cannot increase their total production by doing so. Acting either independently or cooperatively, Robyn will produce 20 coconuts per week and Robinson will produce a total of 10 fish or coconuts per week.

Robyn benefits substantially in this situation because she can fully specialize and earn large gains from trade. Robinson does not benefit because the terms of trade equal his cost trade-offs. Cooperation loses its attractiveness because the presence of the market permits Robyn to completely specialize. In contrast, the advantages of cooperation would not necessarily be lost if Robyn and Robinson actually worked together and thereby increased their combined output. In such a situation the presence of a market can further increase the gains of cooperation.

The terms of trade in the nearby market determine both the activity which will be more profitable and the individual who will benefit the most. For example, if the exchange rate changed to 1 fish for 5 coconuts, both Robyn and Robinson would devote all their work time to fishing. However, the latter would be better off than the former since he can catch twice as many fish.

Important Concepts

Market Demand Curve
Market Supply Curve
Market Equilibrium
Excess Demand
Excess Supply
Equilibrium Price
Equilibrium Quantity
Total Revenue
Elasticity of Supply
Elasticity of Demand
Substitutability
Relative Importance to Consumer
Short Run
Technological Change
Cross Elasticity of Demand
Substitute
Complement
Transportation Costs
Market
Technology

2
The Great American Orange
Characteristics of a National Market

Oranges are an important fruit favored by many Americans. They are grown on trees which do not bear fruit until several years after planting. The American orange industry is centered in three states: Texas, California, and Florida. Assume in this chapter that essentially all the nation's oranges are produced in these states and that each state is a major producer.

Oranges are sold in a series of interrelated regional markets. Assume that together these markets form an integrated national market in which the wholesale price of oranges is the same throughout the country except for differences due to transportation costs. That is, the price of oranges in Boston differs from the price in New York City only by a small increment required to cover the additional transportation costs.

Further assume that there is only one quality grade of oranges and that California, Texas, and Florida oranges are perfect substitutes for each other. Also assume that the national orange market exhibits the other characteristics of perfect competition—many buyers and sellers, freedom of entry and exit for buyers and sellers, and widespread knowledge among buyers and sellers of one another's actions.

1. The demand curve in any market indicates the quantities of the good that buyers are willing to purchase at different prices. Analogously, the supply curve denotes the quantities of the good that producers are willing to sell at different prices. Representative demand and supply curves for the national orange market are shown in Figure 2–1. Presuming that no major changes occur, indicate in the figure the price of oranges that will prevail at equilibrium. Also indicate the quantity of oranges that will be sold at equilibrium.

Figure 2-1

Equilibrium in the Orange Market

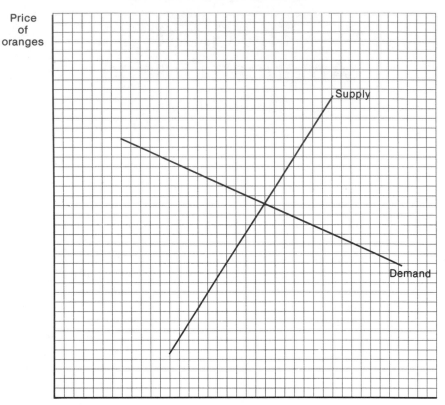

Price
of
oranges

Quantity of oranges

2. In intuitive terms, the price elasticity of demand depicts the responsiveness of the quantity demanded to changes in price. Specifically, it is defined as the percentage change in the quantity demanded divided by the percentage change in price. The price elasticity of supply is defined analogously. For succinctness and reflecting to a large extent customary usage, in this book the price elasticity of demand will be termed simply the elasticity of demand. Correspondingly, the price elasticity of supply will be referred to as the elasticity of supply.

Based on the information supplied and general knowledge about oranges, what will be the approximate elasticity of the demand for oranges over a time period of one year? That is, will demand be very elastic, moderately elastic, etc.? What will be the approximate elasticity of the supply of oranges during the same time period?

3. An inexpensive new hormone is introduced which increases the percentage of orange blossoms maturing into oranges. This hormone is equally accessible to orange growers in the three states. What will be the impact of this development on the variables shown below over the course of one year? Total revenue is defined as the price of oranges multiplied by the quantity of oranges sold.

- price of oranges;
- quantity of oranges sold in the United States;
- quantity of oranges sold by Texas growers;
- quantity of oranges sold by Florida growers;
- quantity of oranges sold by California growers;
- total revenue of American orange growers;
- total revenue of Texas orange growers;
- total revenue of Florida orange growers;
- total revenue of California orange growers.

4. A freeze in Florida and Texas destroys a significant part of the orange crop in those states. The freeze damage is similar in the two areas. What will be the impact of this event on the variables specified in the previous question over a one-year period?

5. The freight rates on goods shipped from California are significantly raised by railroads and truckers—an action affecting a wide range of products, including oranges and other citrus fruits. What will be the impact of this rate increase on the variables specified in Question 3 over a one-year period?

6. A rapidly spreading plant disease substantially reduces the nation's apple crop. What will be the impact of this apple disease on the variables specified in Question 3 over a one-year period?

7. Because of their location, a cluster of orange growers in southern Florida manages to endure the recent freeze without appreciable damage to their crops. What will be the effect of the freeze on the total revenue of these Florida growers?

8. For personal as opposed to business reasons, an individual Texas grower decides not to employ the new hormone described above. If the hormone is widely used in the orange industry, what will be the effect of this grower's decision on his total revenue?

9. June Flynn lives in a small California town and purchases oranges at a local orchard, while Alan Schwartz, residing in Florida, buys oranges at a local orchard there. If freight rates on California oranges increase as described above, what will be the impact on the respective prices paid by Flynn and Schwartz?

DISCUSSION

1. In the natural sciences, equilibrium is defined as the state when there is no tendency for net change. This does not mean that there is no movement of elements within the system, but rather that forces acting in one direction are balanced by equal forces operating in the opposite direction. Equilibrium is defined analogously in economics. A market is at equilibrium if there is no systematic tendency for the price or quantity to change.

The representative demand and supply curves for the national orange market are displayed in Figure 2–2. When will this market be at equilibrium? To respond to this question, begin by assuming that the price of oranges is initially P_1. At that price the quantity buyers are willing to purchase is Q_1, and the quantity suppliers are willing to sell is Q_2. Since Q_2 exceeds Q_1, excess supply exists. Whenever this is true there is a systematic tendency for price to decline as sellers vie with each other for buyers. As price falls, the quantity suppliers are willing to sell decreases while the quantity buyers are willing to purchase increases. Excess supply thus contracts as price declines. Eventually the price P_0 is reached; at that price the quantity supplied equals the quantity demanded. Excess supply has therefore vanished and a systematic tendency for price to fall no longer exists.

Now assume that the initial price is not P_1, but rather P_2. At this price the quantity demanded equals Q_4, while the quantity supplied equals Q_3. Because Q_4 is larger than Q_3, excess demand now characterizes the orange market. Whenever excess demand exists, there is a systematic tendency for price to rise as buyers compete with each other for sellers. As price increases, the quantity demanded falls while the quantity supplied rises. Once again this process continues until the price P_0 is reached. As noted above, at that price the quantity demanded equals the quantity supplied. Excess demand is thus no longer present, and there is no systematic tendency for price to increase.

Equilibrium therefore occurs in the national orange market when the price is P_0. When this is true, there is no systematic tendency for price or

Figure 2-2

Equilibrium in the Orange Market

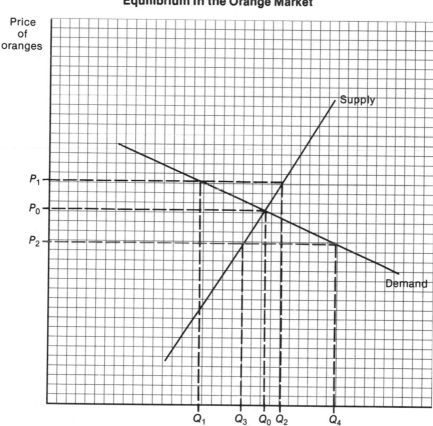

quantity to change in either direction. The quantity of oranges that will be sold at equilibrium is thus Q_0.

In this case the relevant market is nationwide, consisting of interrelated regional markets. Markets are often both this large and this complex. However, this need not be so. For example, the market for water in a small isolated community may consist of a single seller and thirty or forty buyers.

2. The most important determinant of demand elasticity for any product is the number and similarity of possible substitutes. The greater the degree of substitutability, the more elastic will be demand. While oranges are a distinctive fruit, much beloved by some people, there are still many substitutes available, including a wide range of fruits, as well as tomatoes in the consumption of juice. Further, an individual can decrease fruit consumption and increase consumption of other foods. Oranges are thus characterized by relatively high substitutability.

A less important but still significant determinant of demand elasticity is the relative importance of the good to the consumer. If expenditures for a good comprise only a very small fraction of the consumer's budget, purchases will be less influenced by price. Oranges occupy a small but still appreciable position in the consumer's food budget. On the one hand, oranges are not beef, but on the other, they are not vanilla extract.

What will be the net impact of these two factors? The substitutability effect will dominate and will make demand elastic. This influence will be mitigated to some extent by the small but not tiny importance of oranges to the consumer. The result will be that the demand for oranges will be moderately elastic over a one-year time period.

Orange trees must be cultivated for several years before they bear fruit. It will also be difficult in a one-year time frame to significantly change certain other inputs, such as specialized equipment. These factors make the supply of oranges relatively inelastic during the one-year period. However, supply will not be completely inelastic since even over this time frame the quantity of oranges offered for sale may increase or decrease through such actions as adjustments in inventories and changes in harvesting practices.

The one-year time period in this case is an example of the short run. On the production side in the short run some inputs are variable, but others are not, as is true here. On the consumption side fewer options are open to consumers in the short run than in the long run. As a result, although the supply of oranges in this situation is inelastic while the demand for oranges is elastic, both are less elastic than they would be over a longer time frame. This illustrates the general point that another important determinant of demand and supply elasticity is the time period involved.

3. As shown in Figure 2–3, the original demand and supply curves in the national orange market are D_0 and S_0 respectively. The initial price is P_0 and the initial quantity is Q_0. The introduction of the new hormone will decrease the cost of growing oranges. As a result, suppliers will be willing to offer the same numbers of oranges but at lower prices. That is, the supply curve for oranges will shift downward to the right. The post-hormone supply curve is thus S_1 with equilibrium occurring at a price of P_1 and at a quantity of Q_1.

The impact of the hormone's introduction is therefore to decrease the price of oranges and to increase the quantity sold. The increase in

Figure 2-3

Impact of Hormone Introduction: National Market

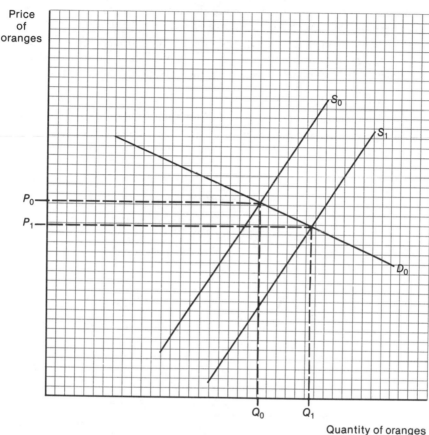

quantity will occur in all three states since the hormone is equally accessible to orange growers in the three areas. Since the price of oranges decreases while the quantity increases, the impact on total revenue will depend upon the elasticity of demand. Since the demand for oranges over a one-year period is elastic for the reasons discussed earlier, the total revenue of orange growers will rise, and this increase will be experienced in all three states.

The discovery and use of the new hormone is an example of a change in technology. Technology is defined as the total existing body of knowledge which may be applied to industrial, commerical, agricultural, or related objectives. To be accepted, a technological change must be either cost-reducing or quality-enhancing. The new hormone is a cost-reducing

23

innovation since there is no indication that the quality of oranges is improved through the hormone's use. Some innovations decrease costs but also reduce quality, while others increase both quality and cost. Prominent examples of the latter are the complex therapies which have been recently developed for the treatment of human illness, e.g., kidney dialysis, cancer chemotherapy, and open-heart surgery. That is, these types of treatment raise the quality of medical care by prolonging or improving life in certain instances, but they are highly expensive.

4. The freeze damage in Florida and Texas will reduce the quantity of oranges which sellers are willing to offer at each price. Thus, as illustrated in Figure 2–4, the supply curve will shift upward to the left,

Figure 2-4

Impact of Freeze: National Market

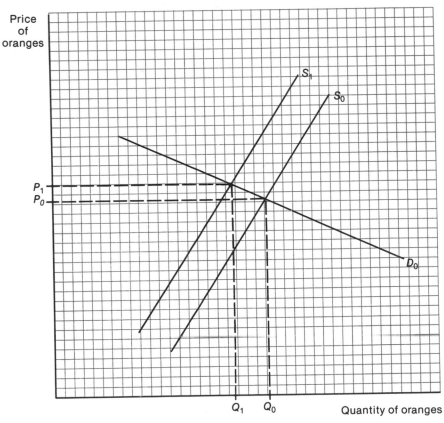

Figure 2-5

Impact of Freeze: California Market

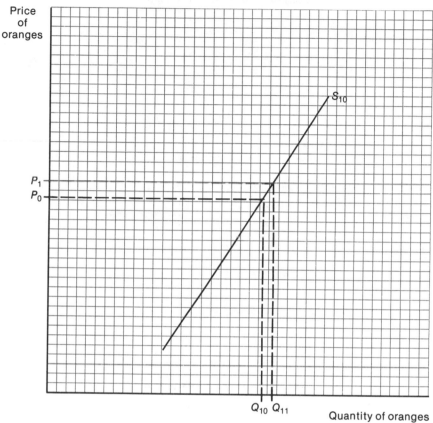

the price of oranges will increase, and the quantity sold in the United States will fall. The total revenue of American orange growers will thus depend upon the elasticity of demand for oranges. Since demand is elastic, total revenue will fall.

After the freeze in Florida and Texas, California orange growers will be willing to sell more oranges at the new higher price of P_1. As illustrated in Figure 2–5, at the new equilibrium they will sell more oranges and their total revenue will rise since both the price of oranges and the quantity of oranges marketed by them will increase.

In Florida and Texas the partial destruction of the orange crops will produce an upward shift in the regional supply curves, as depicted in Figures 2–6 and 2–7. Growers in these states will therefore sell fewer oranges than before. At the new equilibrium in Florida and Texas, price

Figure 2-6

Impact of Freeze: Florida Market

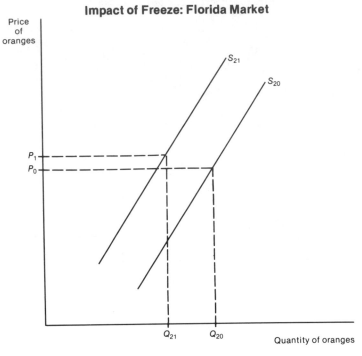

Figure 2-7

Impact of Freeze: Texas Market

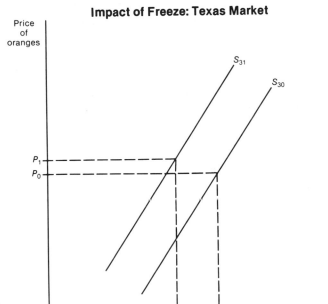

will thus be higher but quantity will be lower. Hence, the impact on total revenue could be uncertain, but this is not in fact true. As discussed above, the total revenue of all American growers will decline and the total revenue of California growers will increase. Given these two results, the total revenue of Texas and Florida growers must decrease.

5. The rise in freight rates will increase the cost of oranges sold by California growers. Hence, as shown in Figures 2–8 through 2–11, the national supply curve and the California supply curve will shift upward, but the Florida and Texas supply curves will not change. At the national level the price of oranges will increase and the quantity sold will decline. Since demand is elastic, total revenue will fall. The quantity of oranges sold by California growers will decline as will their total revenue. In contrast, the quantity of oranges sold by Texas and Florida growers will increase. This result coupled with the price rise will raise the total revenue of the growers in these two states.

This case and the previous one illustrate the general premise that damage to a substantial subset of producers will benefit the other producers in the industry. The damage may be physical as in the case of the freeze, or it may be financial as is true here. In either case the results are the same: Those producers affected lose and those producers not affected gain.

Figure 2-8

Impact of Freight Rate Increase: National Market

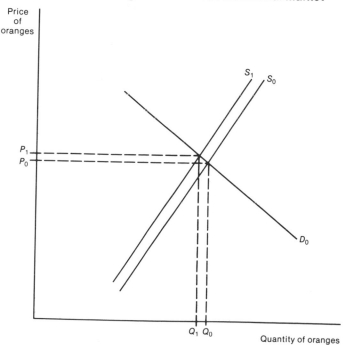

27

Figure 2-9

Impact of Freight Rate Increase: California Market

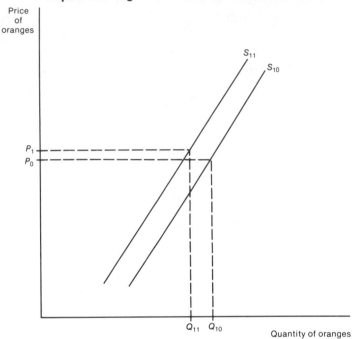

Figure 2-10

Impact of Freight Rate Increase: Florida Market

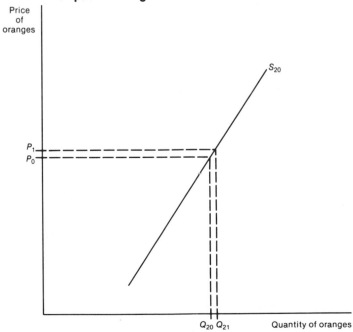

Figure 2-11

Impact of Freight Rate Increase: Texas Market

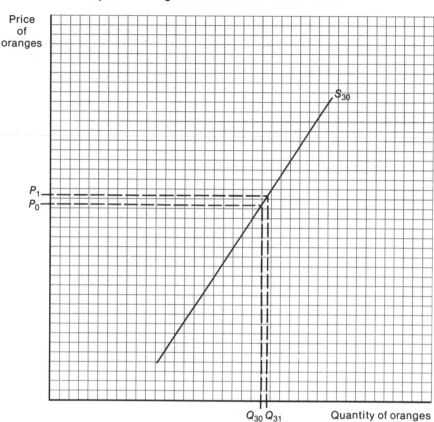

6. The plant disease which afflicts the nation's apples will shift the apple supply curve upward. As a result, the price of apples will rise. Since apples are an important substitute for oranges, the demand curve for oranges will shift upward to the right, thereby increasing the price and quantity of oranges sold. These changes, depicted in Figure 2–12, will apply to orange growers in all three states. Since both the price and quantity of oranges will rise, the total revenue of growers will increase.

The situation in the apple market is presented in Figure 2–13. Initial equilibrium occurs at the intersection of the original supply and demand curves, where the price is P_{40} and the quantity Q_{40}. As described above, the supply curve moves upward because of the plant disease. An additional change is that the demand curve also shifts upward, albeit not to

29

Figure 2-12

Impact of Apple Disease: National Orange Market

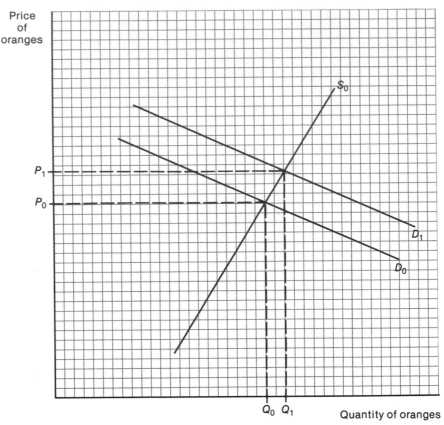

the same extent. The reason is the increase in the price of oranges, which are a substitute for apples as apples are for oranges. The result of these supply and demand changes is that the price of apples will be higher and the quantity lower.

The cross elasticity of demand is defined analogously to the price elasticity. It equals the percentage change in the quantity demanded of one good produced by a percentage change in the price of another good. If the cross elasticity of demand is positive for two goods, the goods are substitutes. This is the case here. An increase in the price of apples raises the demand for oranges. Conversely, a rise in the price of oranges increases the demand for apples.

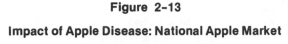

Figure 2-13

Impact of Apple Disease: National Apple Market

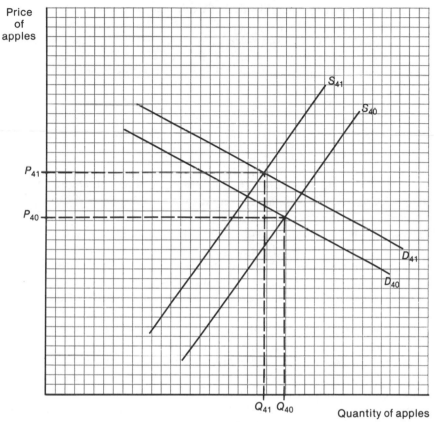

If the cross elasticity of demand is negative, the goods are complements. As implied by the term, complements are used together for a
common purpose, with an excellent example being cars and tires.
Complements are much less common than substitutes. Illustrating this
point, oranges and certain products are used in a complementary fashion,
but the relationship is too weak for a change in the price of one product
to appreciable affect the demand for the other. That is, the cross elasticity
of demand for the two goods approximates zero. For example, oranges
and vodka are used as complements to make screwdrivers. However, it
is most unlikely that an increase in the price of vodka will significantly
influence the demand for oranges.

7. As discussed earlier, the freeze leads to an increase in the price of oranges. Since the crop of these growers is not affected by the freeze, they will sell at least as many oranges as before but at a higher price. Hence, their total revenue, like that of California growers, will increase.

8. In this situation the price of oranges will fall. This individual grower will produce approximately the same number of oranges as before, but will only be able to sell them at the lower price. His total revenue will therefore decline.

This example illustrates the general point that if an individual producer chooses not to use a significant technological innovation, his total revenue will usually fall. As a result, he may be forced to leave the industry if he continues to ignore the technological advance.

9. In this situation the national price of oranges, including transportation costs, will rise. Since freight rates on Florida and Texas products have not increased, the orange prices received by Texas and Florida growers at their orchards must be higher. Hence, Alan Schwartz will now have to pay a higher price for oranges at local Florida orchards.

As shown in Figure 2–9, the supply curve for California oranges will shift upward in this situation. The magnitude of the shift equals the increase in freight rates. However, the increase in the price of oranges is much less than the upward shift in the California supply curve. Two factors are responsible for this result. First, the demand for oranges is elastic while the supply is inelastic. If the reverse characteristics held, i.e., if demand were inelastic and supply were elastic, the rise in price would more nearly approximate the increase in freight rates. Second, the change in the national supply curve is less than the shift in the California supply curve because the costs of Florida and Texas oranges are not influenced by the rise in freight rates.

The situation within California is depicted in Figure 2–14. As in Figure 2–9, P_0 is the initial equilibrium price for oranges and P_1 is the new equilibrium price. The difference between P_1 and P_2 is the increase in freight rates. P_2 is thus the price received by California growers, exclusive of the change in freight rates. This price is lower than the initial equilibrium price. Consequently, June Flynn as a consumer of oranges will be better off than before since orange prices at local California orchards will decline.

While the results in this situation may not be immediately obvious, there is nonetheless a solid rationale underlying them. The change in freight rates decreases the quantity of California oranges demanded in

Figure 2-14

Impact of Freight Rate Increase Within California

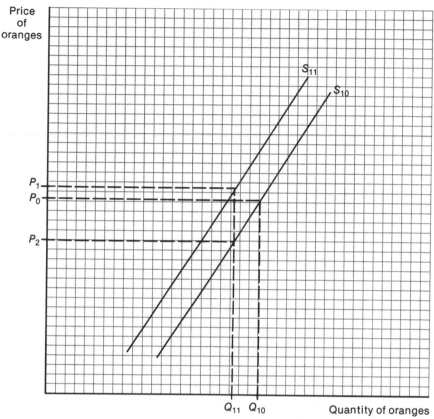

other states and increases the quantity of Florida oranges demanded in other states. As a result, orange prices decline within California, while they increase within Florida.

Important Concepts

Marginality
Opportunity Cost
Marginal Revenue
Marginal Cost
Profit
Fixed Cost
Marginal Gain
Binding Constraint
Nonbinding Constraint
Input Substitutability
Relative Input Prices
Marginal Physical Product
Cash Subsidy Program
Income-in-kind Program
Budget Line
Indifference Curve
Superior Good
Inferior Good
Utility
Principle of Diminishing Marginal Utility
Isoquant
Isocost Curve

3
Who's Measuring What When

Consumer and Producer Decision Making

1. The president of a New York travel agency is considering the addition of a weekly bus tour. Investigation by her staff yields the following information.

- The addition of the tour is expected to increase the company's direct costs by $2,500 per month. Direct costs encompass the expenses of such items as labor, gasoline, and vehicle maintenance.
- The addition of the tour is expected to increase overhead expenses by $100 per month to a total of $25,100 per month. The accounting staff follows its customary practice of assigning this overhead in equal shares to all of the agency's tours. Since this tour, if approved, would be the 50th, the staff allocates $502 per month in overhead to it.
- The monthly revenue from the new tour is expected to equal $2,800.
- During the last five years the agency's total revenues have consistently exceeded its total costs.

Should the agency's president, interested in maximizing the company's profits, approve the new tour?

2. Jennifer is a college student in Massachusetts. She is studying for final examinations, all of which will be held tomorrow. After reviewing her alternatives, she has decided to spend five hours studying this evening. She has also determined that it would be unwise to spend any time studying tomorrow.

Jennifer's objective is to maximize the total of her examination scores in her four courses—philosophy, French, economics, and accounting.

She estimates that additional study hours will increase her examination scores in the manner shown in Table 3–1.

  a. As suggested by its name, the opportunity cost of a given action is defined as the gain that is foregone by pursuing that action rather than others. For example, in Chapter 1 Robinson Crusoe's opportunity cost of spending one hour catching fish is the four coconuts that he could have picked during that time.

  Given this definition, what opportunity cost does Jennifer incur by spending the first hour studying French? In light of this cost, should she spend that hour in this pursuit?

  b. How should she allocate the five hours of study time?

  c. Suppose Jennifer were to have the misfortune of inadvertently leaving her accounting books and notes in a locked classroom at school. Since it would be most difficult to retrieve these materials this evening, it would be impossible for Jennifer to study accounting. If this event were to occur, what would be the impact on the optimal allocation of Jennifer's study time?

  d. An examination grade less than 65 is considered a failing mark at the college Jennifer attends. Bearing this point in mind, she further considers her optimal strategy. She decides that to insure against the possibility of failing any examination, she should allocate her study time so as to maximize her estimated total points in the four examinations, but subject to the constraint that her estimated points on each examination must be at least 70. How should Jennifer now allocate her study time? Presume in this instance that Jennifer did not misplace her accounting materials as postulated in the previous question.

Table 3-1

Effects of Additional Study

Additional Study Hours	Estimated Total Points on Each Examination			
	Philosophy	French	Economics	Accounting
0	80	65	70	82
1	90	69	72	85
2	95	71	77	88
3	97	73	82	90
4	98	73	86	92
5	99	74	88	93

3. A real estate agent from Georgia is in the midst of a month-long trip through India. In the course of her travels she writes a letter to a friend in Atlanta, excerpts of which follow.

> Yesterday we drove from Delhi to Agra and were repeatedly delayed by road construction. Since we were stopped at several detours for twenty or thirty minutes, I had the opportunity to observe how the Indians build roads.
>
> Women came streaming by carrying rocks in baskets on their heads. Men were digging drainage ditches along the road, often with primitive tools. Concrete was poured by workers using hand machines.
>
> This experience has helped me to understand that Western technology is still poorly understood in India. It seems clear that India's economic position would be greatly improved if the country relied more heavily on capital equipment to do the jobs now being inefficiently performed by hand labor.

Is the Georgian's conclusion sound?

4. Two types of programs have been the primary vehicles used to reduce poverty in the United States. One, termed the cash subsidy program, entails giving the poor cash payments which they may spend as they think best. The other, termed the income-in-kind program, involves providing specific kinds of assistance, such as furnishing free food or medical care.

A Michigan welfare agency is considering two alternative programs—one a cash subsidy program and the other an income-in-kind program. Its resources will permit the addition of one but not both programs. Those eligible for either program would be families earning less than $6,600 per year or $550 per month. Program *A* is the cash subsidy program; it would provide an eligible family with an unrestricted cash payment of $120 per month. Under the income-in-kind program, Program *B*, an eligible family would receive a rent subsidy up to $120 per month. That is, the agency would reimburse each family for that portion of its monthly rental bill which did not exceed $120.

a. Will Program *A* improve the housing conditions of eligible families?

b. Will Program *B* increase the expenditures by eligible families for goods and services other than housing?

c. In this setting a budget line shows the maximum possible combinations of housing and other commodities that can be consumed by the typical recipient family in a given situation. An indifference curve depicts the combinations of housing and other commodities, among which the

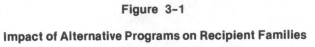

Figure 3-1

Impact of Alternative Programs on Recipient Families

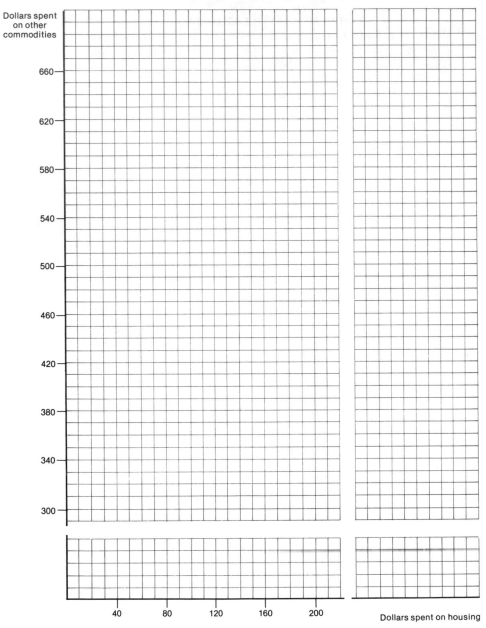

family is indifferent. As the family moves along a given indifference curve, its level of utility remains unchanged. In contrast, as the family shifts from one indifference curve to another, its utility changes. As defined in economics, utility is essentially synonymous with satisfaction, but satisfaction in a broad sense. That is, an individual can gain utility by sleeping, painting a picture, watching television, embracing another person, or eating a lobster.

As a base for further analysis, draw in Figure 3–1 the budget line for a typical recipient family in the absence of either program. Assume that such a family earns $6,000 per year or $500 per month. Then draw in the same figure the budget line for this family under Program *A*, and the budget line under Program *B*.

Now draw in Figure 3–1 a set of indifference curves for a recipient family which has a low preference for housing. Draw these curves so that the figure will indicate the amounts of housing and other commodities consumed per month by this family in each of the three situations (no program, Program *A*, or Program *B*). Carry out the same procedure for a family with a high preference for housing.

d. If the Michigan agency wishes to maximize the utility or satisfaction of the recipients, which program should it select?

e. If the agency wishes to maximize the improvement in recipients' housing conditions, which program should it select?

f. Which type of recipient family will be relatively indifferent as to which of the programs the agency selects—those with a high preference for housing or those with a low preference?

DISCUSSION

1. Marginal revenue is defined as the additional revenue produced by a given event. In this case the event is the addition of the new tour. Accordingly, marginal revenue will equal $2,800 per month. Marginal cost is defined analogously. In this situation it will include the $2,500 increase in monthly direct costs and the $100 rise in monthly overhead costs. Marginal cost will thus equal $2,600 per month.

The profit arising from a given event equals the marginal revenue of the event minus the marginal cost of the event. In this instance the monthly profit of the new tour will equal $2,800 minus $2,600, or $200. Hence, the tour should be approved. It is also clear that the agency should not be shut down since its total revenues have been consistently greater than its total costs.

The monthly overhead expense of $25,000 is a fixed cost. It must be paid whether or not the new tour is added. This producer, the New York travel agency, should therefore not take it into account in deciding whether to add the tour.

2a. The opportunity cost of spending the first hour studying French is the 10 points Jennifer would have earned by spending that hour on her best alternative, philosophy. In contrast, her gain from such study is only 4 points. The opportunity cost of French study during the first hour is thus greater than the gain achieved. That being the case, she should not elect to study French during that hour.

2b. Jennifer wants to accumulate as many examination points as possible; she therefore allocates her five hours of study time to those subjects where their marginal gains are the greatest. Accordingly, she spends the first two hours studying philosophy, where the marginal gains are 10 and 5 points respectively. Her remaining three hours should be spent studying economics, where the marginal gains are 2, 5, and 5 points respectively. By studying the additional five hours Jennifer thus increases the total of her examination scores by 27 points, i.e., 15 in philosophy and 12 in economics.

Devoting three study hours to economics may seem contradictory since the gain from studying either French or accounting in the third hour is more than 2 points, the number gained by allocating the third study hour to economics. However, allocating the third study hour to French and the fourth and fifth hours to accounting will only increase Jennifer's examination scores by 10 points. In contrast, if Jennifer devotes all three hours to economics, her examination scores will increase by 12 points. The low marginal gain in the first hour of economics study is thus more than compensated by the high marginal gains in the second and third hours.

2c. The temporary loss of Jennifer's accounting books and notes does not affect her optimal studying strategy. As discussed above, her best option is to devote two study hours to philosophy and three to economics. This is true whether or not she has her accounting materials.

The loss of these materials is thus an example of a nonbinding constraint. Such a constraint changes the options open to the decision maker, but does not affect the optimal strategy.

2d. Without further study Jennifer expects to receive an examination score of at least 70 in all subjects except French. She should therefore devote study time to French until she has satisfied the constraint that she must receive a score of at least 70 in that subject. Accordingly, she should devote her first two study hours to French, which will increase her estimated score in that subject to 71.

Now that Jennifer expects to receive a score of at least 70 in each subject, she should allocate her remaining three study hours to those subjects where the marginal gain is the greatest. She should therefore devote her third and fourth hours to philosophy, where the marginal gains are 10 and 5 points respectively; and the fifth hour to accounting, where the marginal gain is 3 points.

In this case by studying the additional five hours Jennifer increases her examination scores by 24 points, i.e., 6 in French, 15 in philosophy, and 3 in accounting. In the previous case her total point gain was 27. The imposition of the constraint that she must attain a score of at least 70 in each subject thus reduces the increase in Jennifer's examination scores by 3 points. That is, the cost of satisfying this constraint is the loss of 3 points.

This case illustrates the effect of a binding constraint. A constraint of this type not only changes the options available, but forces a revision in the optimal strategy. A constrained maximum can never be greater than an unconstrained maximum. More important, except in unusual instances where two options are equally attractive in the unconstrained situation, the constrained maximum will be less than the unconstrained maximum, as is true in Jennifer's case.

3. The first issue to consider in evaluating the Georgian's argument is whether labor and capital are substitutes in the production of roads. If they are not, only a single ratio or proportion of labor to capital can be used to construct roads, and the Georgia real estate agent might be correct on this basis alone. However, instances where labor and capital can only be employed in fixed proportions are rare. This is especially true for aggregate inputs like labor and capital. This general premise holds here. Labor and capital are substitutes, albeit imperfect ones, in the production of roads.

Since the two inputs are substitutes, how should they be combined to efficiently construct roads? As in the previous two questions, the principle of marginality again provides a sound basis for decision making. The marginal physical product of labor (MPP_L) is defined as the increment in road construction resulting from the employment of an additional unit of labor. The marginal physical product of capital (MPP_K) is defined analogously. The price of labor (P_L) and the price of capital (P_K) are respectively the unit costs of labor and capital to the road contractor. Efficient production occurs when the ratio of the marginal physical products equals the ratio of the input prices, i.e., when $MPP_L/MPP_K = P_L/P_K$.

To illustrate this principle, suppose that the ratio of the marginal physical products is four, while the ratio of the input prices is one. A road builder can thus obtain four times as much additional output by adding a unit of labor instead of a unit of capital. Since the cost of adding either unit is the same, it is clearly advantageous to use additional labor rather than additional capital. The converse holds if, for example, the ratio of the marginal physical products is two and the ratio of the input prices is five.

In more intuitive terms, this principle means that a road builder should use most heavily those productive resources which are relatively inexpensive. In the United States as in other developed countries, the price of labor is high compared to the price of capital. The reverse is true in India and other less developed countries. A cost-minimizing road builder should therefore use a relatively large amount of capital in this country, but in India he should employ a relatively large amount of labor.

This point is illustrated by a hypothetical example depicted in Figure 3-2. Suppose that an Indian road builder and an American road builder face the same isoquant Q_0. This curve shows the different combinations of labor and capital that can be used to construct Q_0 quantity of road. Suppose further that the two road builders operate under the same total budget of B_0 dollars. C_I is an isocost curve which depicts the different amounts of labor and capital that can be employed with B_0 dollars at the input prices prevailing in India. Correspondingly, the isocost curve C_A indicates the different combinations of labor and capital that can be employed with B_0 dollars at the input prices prevailing in the United States. C_A is much steeper than C_I because the price of labor relative to the price of capital is far higher in the United States than in India.

To minimize costs, the Indian road builder operates at the point where C_I touches Q_0. He thus employs L_1 units of labor and K_1 units of capital. Similarly, the American road builder minimizes costs by using L_2 units of labor and K_2 units of capital. Hence, faced with the same isoquant and working under the same total budget, the Indian and American road builders use highly dissimilar combinations of labor and capital.

The conclusion of the Georgian is thus erroneous. The observation that Indian road builders are using labor intensively and capital sparingly is not an indictment of Indian practices. It shows that these producers are responding to relative input prices in their country. But, it is true that intensive use of labor does not indicate by itself that Indian road building is done efficiently. To assess this point a more detailed evaluation would be necessary, which would include analysis of production relationships, current practices, input costs, and final product quality.

Figure 3-2

Road Construction in India and the United States

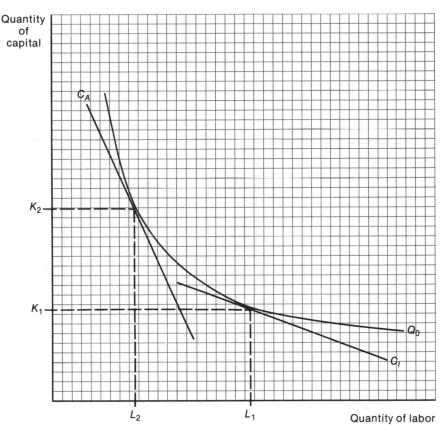

4a. An increase in consumers' income will increase their consumption of most goods and services. There are a few commodities for which this is not true. Termed inferior goods, they are usually specific products. For example, as family income rises, consumption of potatoes and dressmaking patterns may fall. The reason is that the increase in income permits the consumer to substitute preferred goods for the inferior good. That is, the additional income allows the consumer to shift from potatoes and dressmaking patterns toward other foods and manufactured clothing.

As the name suggests, a superior good is a product whose consumption increases as income rises. Essentially all aggregate commodities like food, clothing, or housing are superior goods. Further, consumption of housing by the poor is likely to be quite sensitive to changes in income. Therefore, since Program A, the cash subsidy program, increases the income of eligible families, it will increase their consumption of housing. As a result, their housing conditions will improve.

4b. Program B, the income-in-kind program, will increase the real income of eligible families. In most instances housing will consume a significant portion of this income increase, but it will rarely consume the entirety of the increase. Hence, under Program B, recipients will have additional funds available with which to purchase goods and services other than housing. Put in another way, by providing a rent subsidy Program B frees dollars for other purposes that were previously spent by recipients for housing.

4c. As indicated in Figure 3–3, the budget line for the initial situation (B_0) begins at the point where the family spends its entire monthly income of $500 on other commodities. It then passes downward as the family substitutes housing dollars for dollars spent on other commodities. For example, it passes through the point where the family spends $300 on other commodities and $200 on housing.

The budget line for Program A is the straight line B_A. Since this program increases each family's monthly income by $120 and since the family is free to spend that money on any commodity that it chooses, this line is parallel to B_0 but further from the origin. The budget line for Program B is B_B. Since this program provides a rental subsidy up to $120 but no unrestricted cash, this budget line is parallel to the horizontal axis from the point at which the family spends $500 on other commodities and $0 on housing to the point where it spends $500 on other commodities and $120 on housing. After the family has spent $120 on housing, it must then sacrifice other commodities on a dollar-for-dollar basis in order to obtain more housing. Consequently, beyond $120 of housing the budget line under Program B is identical to that under Program A.

The set of indifference curves for the family with a low preference for housing (termed Family Z) is represented by the dotted lines $I_{Z1}-I_{Z5}$, with the family's utility increasing as it moves from I_{Z1} to I_{Z5}. Initially this family is spending $50 on housing and $450 on other commodities. Under Program A this family spends $90 on housing and $530 on other commodities; under Program B it consumes $120 of housing and $500 of other commodities.

The set of indifference curves for the family with a high preference for housing (termed Family Y) is represented by the solid lines $I_{Y1}-I_{Y5}$, with utility again increasing as the family shifts from I_{Y1} to I_{Y5}. In the

Figure 3-3

Impact of Alternative Programs on Recipient Families

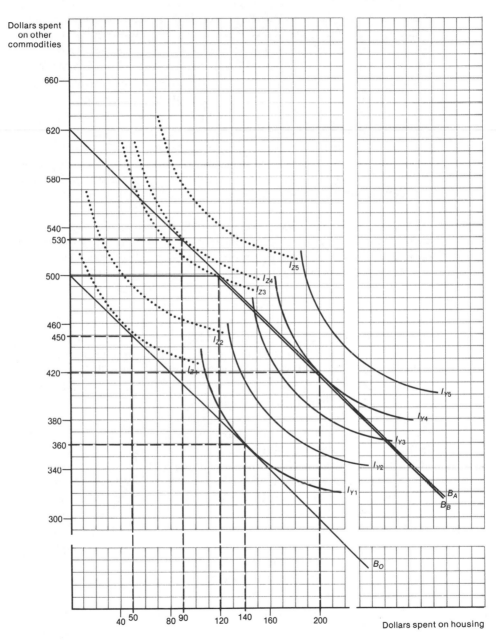

original situation this family consumed $140 of housing and $360 of other commodities. Under either Program A or Program B it spends $200 on housing and $420 on other commodities.

The indifference curves in Figure 3–3 reflect a central element in consumer theory—the principle of diminishing marginal utility. This principle holds that as the consumption of a commodity increases, with the consumption of other goods held constant, the marginal utility gained will eventually decline. It is this principle which makes the indifference curves in Figure 3–3 convex to the origin. This convexity means that as the ratio of housing consumption to other consumption increases, the consumer is progressively less willing to substitute housing for other goods. The reason is that as this ratio increases, the marginal utility of housing consumption declines while the marginal utility of other consumption increases. Conversely, as this ratio decreases, the marginal utility of housing consumption rises and the marginal utility of other consumption falls.

4d. The budget line represents the consumption opportunity frontier for the recipient family in a given situation. As is evident in Figure 3–3, budget line B_A includes all the points encompassed by budget line B_B as well as a substantial number of additional points. Therefore, in terms of its own preferences the family cannot be worse off under Program A than under Program B. Further, it may be better off under the former than under the latter. This possibility is illustrated by Family Z. Under Program A this family is on a higher indifference curve than it is under Program B. Accordingly, in terms of its own preferences, its utility is higher under Program A than under Program B. Thus, if the Michigan agency's goal is to maximize eligible consumers' satisfaction in their own eyes, it should choose Program A.

4e. Program B not only increases the real income of recipient families, but it also specifically subsidizes housing. To attain the full $120 increase in monthly income, a family must spend as least that amount on housing. Accordingly, a family will not spend less on housing under Program B than under Program A, and it may spend more. Again, Family Z serves as a representative example. Under Program A this family spends $90 per month on housing, whereas under Program B it spends $120. The Michigan agency should thus choose Program B if its main objective is to increase the housing consumption of eligible consumers and to thereby improve their housing conditions.

4f. Families with a high preference for housing will be largely indifferent between the two programs. Under either program they are likely to spend more than $120 per month on housing. As a consequence, the two programs will have the same effects on them. This situation is illustrated by Family *Y*. Under either Program *A* or Program *B* it spends $200 per month on housing and $420 on other commodities.

In contrast, families like Family *Z* with a low preference for housing will prefer Program *A* to Program *B*. As noted earlier, this family consumes more housing under Program *B*, but its satisfaction level is higher under Program *A*.

A further point of interest is to reconsider Questions 4*a* and 4*b* in light of Figure 3–3. In accord with the conclusion reached in Question 4*a*, both Family *Y* and Family *Z* will consume more housing under Program *A* than they do in the original situation. Family *Y* will increase its monthly housing expenditures from $140 to $200, while Family *Z* will increase its expenditures from $50 to $90. In Question 4*b* the point was made that under Program *B* families will increase their expenditures for other commodities. Both of the representative families will also exhibit this characteristic. Family *Y* will increase its monthly expenditures for other commodities from $360 to $420, and Family *Z* will increase its expenditures from $450 to $500.

Important Concepts

Profit Maximization
Entrepreneur
Output Mix
Input Substitutability
Production Function
Relative Input Intensity
Total Revenue
Total Variable Cost
Short-run Profit
Time Horizon
Signalling Function of Prices
Invisible Hand
Law of Diminishing Returns
Fixed Input
Variable Input
Marginal Physical Product
Average Physical Product
Implicit Wage
Work Satisfaction
Implicit Costs
Economic Profit
Accounting Profit
Inferior Production Option

4

The Baker
as an Entrepreneur

Profit Maximization
with Two Outputs

Dmitri Filippov, the profit-maximizing owner/operator of the Poltava
Bakery, is considering his production plans for the next month. The
Poltava is a small bakery which Dmitri bought five years ago. At that
time Dmitri made a sizable down payment, obtaining a mortgage to
cover the rest of the purchase price. His monthly mortgage payment is
now $600; it does not vary with the output of the bakery.

Dmitri is able to produce two kinds of cookies—coconut macaroons
and iced gingerbread people. He sells the cookies on the wholesale
market at the prevailing market prices for macaroons and gingerbread
people. Since the Poltava is small relative to this large market, Dmitri is
able to sell at the current market prices as many batches of cookies as he
produces.

Dmitri owns a number of utensils which are well suited to the production of either macaroons or gingerbread people. He does not intend to
either buy or sell bakery utensils during the next month. Similarly, he
has no plans for selling his bakery or for purchasing another one during
this time period.

The Poltava Bakery is located in Charlestown, a community within the
New York metropolitan area. In general, unionization is strong in New
York, and this characteristic holds in the baking industry. Dmitri thus
uses union labor when he needs bakers' assistants. He can hire as many
bakers' assistants as he desires at the current union wages, which are: $6
per hour during the morning shift, $8 per hour during the afternoon
shift, and $9 per hour during the night shift. Each of these shifts is eight
hours in length. Union bakers' assistants cannot be hired for shorter time
periods than an eight-hour shift, but they can be employed for single
days.

Dmitri must receive an implicit wage of at least $2 per hour to induce him to work during the morning shift. That is, while Dmitri does not explicitly pay himself a wage, he values the alternative uses of his time at $2 per hour during the morning shift. He therefore must include the eight hours of his time valued at the $2 hourly figure in his variable costs. Since after working one shift Dmitri places a higher value on other uses of his time, he will only work the afternoon shift if he receives an implicit wage equal to at least $15 per hour. For similar reasons, he will only work the third shift if he receives an implicit wage of at least $40 per hour.

Given his present stock of capital equipment, Dmitri estimates that the production options shown in Table 4−1 characterize his bakery's production function during the morning shift of each day. In this table

Table 4-1

Production Function for Poltava Bakery

Production Option	Bakers' Assistants per Shift	Cost of Ingredients per Shift	Cost of Using Oven and Utensils per Shift	Cookie Batches per Shift
A	0 (Dmitri only)	$24.15	$5.01	23 M
B	,,	22.30	4.68	16 M 6 G
C	,,	16.45	3.51	8 M 9 G
D	,,	14.60	3.00	16 G
E	1 (plus Dmitri)	25.20	5.24	24 M
F	,,	27.85	6.01	16 M 13 G
G	,,	33.25	7.33	8 M 29 G
H	,,	30.60	6.90	36 G
I	2 (plus Dmitri)	25.20	5.24	24 M
J	,,	27.85	6.01	16 M 13 G
K	,,	33.25	7.33	8 M 29 G
L	,,	40.80	9.18	48 G
M	3 or more (plus Dmitri)	Same input/output combinations as 2 bakers' assistants plus Dmitri.		

the abbreviations "M" and "G" stand for macaroons and gingerbread people respectively.

Dmitri indicates that production data is much less firm for the afternoon shift than for the morning shift. Even so, he thinks that the cost savings gained by being able to plan over a 16-hour period are about offset by the decrease in his productivity caused by fatigue during the second shift. He therefore feels that his bakery's production function is approximately the same for the afternoon shift as for the morning shift.

Dmitri is much less certain about the production schedule that would characterize his bakery during the night shift. However, at a minimum it is clear that he would be extremely tired if he worked three shifts per day and that he would have to sleep during at least part of the night shift. Production at each level of input usage would thus be considerably lower than the outputs shown in Table 4–1.

1. Does the production function of the Poltava Bakery, displayed in Table 4–1, reflect the law of diminishing returns?

2. Making the legitimate presumption that the wage of bakers' assistants will always be greater than zero, are there production options in Table 4–1 which Dmitri should never employ? If so, identify these inferior options.

3. If the price of macaroons is $2.50 per batch and if the price of gingerbread people is $3.00 per batch, how many batches of each should Dmitri produce during the morning shift each day? How many bakers' assistants should he hire? What will be Dmitri's short-run profit (defined throughout this chapter as the difference between total revenue and total variable costs)?

4. If the price of macaroons remains $2.50 per batch and if the price of gingerbread people increases to $5.00 per batch, how many batches of each should Dmitri produce during the morning shift of each day? How many bakers' assistants should he hire? What will Dmitri's profit be?

5. If the price of gingerbread people is $3.00 per batch (as in the initial situation), but the price of macaroons increases to $4.00 per batch, how many batches of each should Dmitri produce during the morning shift of each day? How many bakers' assistants should he hire? What will Dmitri's profit be?

6. If the price of both macaroons and gingerbread people increases to $5.00 per batch, how many batches of each should Dmitri produce during the morning shift of each day? How many bakers' assistants should he hire? What will Dmitri's profit be?

7. Should Dmitri operate his bakery during the afternoon shift at any of the cookie prices described above? Should he operate the bakery during the night shift at any of these prices?

8. Dmitri is offered a job as a baker by another firm at a wage of $10 per hour for the morning shift. However, Dmitri feels that his work satisfaction would be lower in this new position. He therefore would prefer to operate his own bakery if he can earn an implicit wage of at least $7 per hour. At which of the previous cookie prices should Dmitri refuse the job offer and continue to operate his bakery? At which should he take the alternative job and shut down his bakery?

9. Four months have now passed. Dmitri is again considering his production plans for the next month. His cost and production schedules are unchanged except that in the interim the union has negotiated a new agreement with New York bakeries. Under its terms, bakers' assistants will receive $8 per hour during the morning shift, $10 per hour during the afternoon shift, and $11 per hour during the night shift.

Faced with these increased labor costs, and at a price of $5.00 per batch for both macaroons and gingerbread people, how many batches of each should Dmitri produce during the morning shift? How many bakers' assistants should he hire? What will Dmitri's profit be?

10. The word entrepreneur is derived from the French verb *entreprendre,* which means to undertake. A frequent dictionary definition of an entrepreneur is "a person who organizes, operates, and assumes the risk for business ventures." The customary economics definition is an individual who receives as income the residual or difference between the firm's revenues and its payments to other individuals for their goods or services. Given these definitions, is Dmitri an entrepreneur?

DISCUSSION

1. The law of diminishing returns states that if units of an input are progressively added to a production process, with the amount of at least one other input held constant and with technology remaining unchanged, the marginal physical product of the increasing input will eventually decline. In this situation there is an important fixed input—the bakery and its oven. There are several variable inputs, but the one which most reflects the law of diminishing returns is labor. The impact of this law is evident in the production of both macaroons and gingerbread people.

Assuming that Dmitri and the bakers' assistants are sufficiently similar that they can be grouped as labor, the marginal physical product of labor in gingerbread production is 16 batches when only Dmitri works. That is, it equals the 16 batches that can be produced by Dmitri alone minus the zero batches that result when the bakery is shut down. With the addition of the first bakers' assistant, the marginal product of labor rises to 20 batches of gingerbread people. It then declines to 12 batches with the use of the second bakers' assistant, and to zero batches with the employment of additional bakers' assistants.

The Poltava's production function for gingerbread people thus manifests, albeit in abbreviated form, both the stage of increasing returns (when marginal product is rising) and the stage of decreasing returns (when marginal product is falling). The third stage of absolutely decreasing returns (when marginal product is not only falling, but is also negative) is not apparent in Table 4–1, but would almost certainly arise if Dmitri continued to add bakers' assistants.

Since macaroon production is more oven intensive than is gingerbread people production, the stage of increasing returns is not evident and the stage of diminishing returns is short. The marginal product of labor equals 23 batches of macaroons when Dmitri works alone. It then decreases drastically to 1 batch with the employment of one bakers' assistant, and to zero batches with the use of additional bakers' assistants.

The average physical product of labor is defined as the total output divided by the number of workers. Since the marginal product reflects the law of diminishing returns, the average product does as well. In gingerbread people production, the average product initially equals 16 batches. It rises to 18 batches with the use of one bakers' assistant, and it declines thereafter as more bakers' assistants are employed. In macaroon production the decrease in average product is more abrupt. When Dmitri works alone the average product is 23 batches. It declines to 12 batches with the addition of the first bakers' assistant, and to 8 batches with the employment of the second.

2. As discussed in part above, the marginal product of labor is zero for the addition of the second bakers' assistant unless the bakery is producing only gingerbread people. Therefore, as long as the bakers' assistant wage is positive, production options I, J, and K are inferior and should not be used. Similarly, all options employing three or more bakers' assistants are inferior.

3. The total revenue of each production option equals the sum of macaroon revenue and gingerbread people revenue. The former equals the number of macaroon batches produced multiplied by the macaroon price per batch. The latter is defined analogously. As an example, the total revenue of Option K is $107.00, i.e., 8 batches of macaroons times $2.50 plus 29 batches of gingerbread people times $3.00.

Total variable cost includes only those expenses which vary during the time horizon of one month. Accordingly, the monthly mortgage payment is not a component of variable cost. Rather, it is a fixed cost since it remains the same regardless of the output of the bakery. Similarly, the opportunity costs of owning the utensils and the bakery are not included in total variable cost since Dmitri has no intention of selling either during the month time frame.

However, there are several costs which do vary with output during this time horizon and which are thus components of total variable cost. There are three such costs for those production options not employing bakers' assistants: the cost of Dmitri's time which is valued at an implicit wage of $2 per hour; the cost of the ingredients used; and the expenses of using the oven and utensils. If an option uses one or two bakers' assistants, the wages of these individuals must also be included. Therefore, for example, the total variable cost of Option F is $97.86, which is the

Table 4-2

Initial Situation

Production Option	Total Revenue	Total Variable Cost	Short-Run Profit
A	$ 57.50	$ 45.16	$12.34
B	58.00	42.98	15.02
C	47.00	35.96	11.04
D	48.00	33.60	14.40
E	60.00	94.44	Neg.
F	79.00	97.86	Neg.
G	107.00	104.58	2.42
H	108.00	101.50	6.50
L	144.00	161.98	Neg.

sum of the following components: $16.00 for Dmitri's time, $48.00 for the bakers' assistant's wages, $27.85 for ingredients, and $6.01 for oven/utensil usage.

The total revenue and total variable cost of each production option are shown in Table 4–2, which does not include the inferior options identified earlier. The table also indicates the short-run profit of each option. As specified in the question, short-run profit equals total revenue minus total variable cost, i.e., the difference between columns two and three in the table.

As displayed in the table, Option B produces the highest short-run profit. Since Dmitri is a profit maximizer, he should therefore select this option. During each morning shift he will thus produce 16 batches of macaroons and 6 batches of gingerbread people; he will use no bakers' assistants; and his profit will be $15.02.

4. Table 4–3 depicts this situation; it is calculated in the same fashion as Table 4–2. Inspection of this table shows that the new profit-maximizing option is II, which calls for Dmitri to produce 36 batches of gingerbread people per shift with one bakers' assistant. His profit will be $78.50 per shift.

The increased price of gingerbread people serves as a signal to producers. It informs them that this kind of cookie is now more highly

Table 4-3

Increase in Price of Gingerbread People

Production Option	Total Revenue	Total Variable Cost	Short-Run Profit
A	$ 57.50	$ 45.16	$12.34
B	70.00	42.98	27.02
C	65.00	35.96	29.04
D	80.00	33.60	46.40
E	60.00	94.44	Neg.
F	105.00	97.86	7.14
G	165.00	104.58	60.42
H	180.00	101.50	78.50
L	240.00	161.98	78.02

valued by consumers. Dmitri and other producers can therefore increase their profits by shifting their production from other kinds of cookies to gingerbread people. In so doing they satisfy consumer preferences as well.

Writing more than two hundred years ago, Adam Smith recognized and emphasized this signalling function of prices, which he termed the "invisible hand." The central point in this image is that the market through its price structure provides meaningful information to producers and consumers. It is thus not necessary for consumers to send an emissary to producers telling them that they would like more gingerbread people. Instead, the increase in consumer demand leads to a rise in the price of gingerbread people, which in turn induces producers to supply more cookies of this type.

5. Table 4–4 summarizes the revenue/cost trade-offs in this situation. It indicates that Dmitri's profit-maximizing option is now A, which means that Dmitri will produce 23 batches of macaroons per shift and will employ no bakers' assistants. His profit will be $46.84 per shift.

This case is the mirror image of the previous one. The increase in the macaroon price, as compared to the initial situation, induces Dmitri to shift toward the production of this type of cookie. In fact, analogous to

Table 4-4

Increase in Macaroon Price

Production Option	Total Revenue	Total Variable Cost	Short-Run Profit
A	$ 92.00	$ 45.16	$46.84
B	82.00	42.98	39.02
C	59.00	35.96	23.04
D	48.00	33.60	14.40
E	96.00	94.44	1.56
F	103.00	97.86	5.14
G	119.00	104.58	14.42
H	108.00	101.50	6.50
L	144.00	161.98	Neg.

the previous case where he produced only gingerbread people, his entire output now consists of macaroons.

The shift to the exclusive production of macaroons in turn has an important effect. Macaroon production is more oven intensive and less labor intensive than gingerbread people production. Consequently, when the change in cookie prices signals Dmitri that he should produce only macaroons, he does not find it profitable to hire a bakers' assistant as he did in the previous case when he expanded his production of gingerbread people.

6. As shown in Table 4–5, Dmitri's profit-maximizing option is now G. Accordingly, during each shift he will produce 8 batches of macaroons and 29 batches of gingerbread people, and he will employ one bakers' assistant. Doing this, he will earn a profit of $80.42 per shift.

Compared to the initial situation, both cookie prices have increased in this case. Yet Dmitri does not increase his output of both cookies. Rather, he decreases his production of macaroons from 16 to 8 batches and increases his production of gingerbread people from 6 to 29 batches. What factors explain these seemingly conflicting results?

The underlying cause is the relative input intensity of the two types of cookies. As discussed earlier, macaroon production is more oven inten-

Table 4–5

Increase in Both Cookie Prices

Production Option	Total Revenue	Total Variable Cost	Short-Run Profit
A	$115.00	$ 45.16	$69.84
B	110.00	42.98	67.02
C	85.00	35.96	49.04
D	80.00	33.60	46.40
E	120.00	94.44	25.56
F	145.00	97.86	47.14
G	185.00	104.58	80.42
H	180.00	101.50	78.50
L	240.00	161.98	78.02

sive and less labor intensive than is gingerbread people production. During the month time horizon Dmitri cannot change the amount of oven time available, but he can vary his employment of labor inputs. When Dmitri tries to increase production of both cookies in response to increases in the prices, he soon encounters the oven constraint in the production of macaroons. He therefore shifts his output mix in order to overcome the binding constraint imposed by the fixed input. That is, he hires a bakers' assistant and shifts toward the production of the more labor-intensive cookie, gingerbread people.

7. Since the cookie prices are the same regardless of the shift during which the cookies are produced and since the bakery's production schedule is approximately the same for the afternoon shift as for the morning shift, the total revenue of each production option will be about the same for the two shifts. However, this is not true for total variable cost. The hourly wage for bakers' assistants is $2 higher for the afternoon shift than for the morning shift. More important, the implicit wage that Dmitri feels he must receive is now $15 per hour, rather than $2 per hour.

Total variable cost for all options using no bakers' assistants will thus increase by $104, i.e., 8 hours of Dmitri's time multiplied by $13 per hour. Total variable cost for those options using one bakers' assistant will rise by $120, i.e., $104 for Dmitri plus 8 hours of a bakers' assistant multiplied by $2 per hour; and total variable cost for the option using two bakers' assistants will increase by $136, i.e., $104 for Dmitri plus 16 hours of bakers' assistant multiplied by $2 per hour.

When these additional costs are compared to the profits shown in Tables 4–2 through 4–5, it is evident that the profit of all options would be negative if Dmitri operated during the afternoon shift. He should therefore not do so. Similarly, since costs are even higher and output is lower during the night shift, he should also not operate during this shift.

This question emphasizes the importance of implicit costs. It also points up the difference between economic profits and accounting profits. Consider the possibility of operating the afternoon shift when both cookie prices are $5 per batch. At these prices the preferred production option is G, which yields a total revenue of $185. The explicit costs of this production option during the afternoon shift are now $104.58, i.e., $33.25 for ingredients, $7.33 for oven/utensil usage, and $64.00 for the bakers' assistant's wages. The difference between total revenue and explicit costs is therefore $80.42

Does this mean that Dmitri should operate the afternoon shift? As noted above, the answer is no. The reason is that Dmitri's implicit costs for the afternoon shift are $120 for his labor. Since these implicit costs exceed the difference between total revenue and explicit costs, he should not operate the afternoon shift.

Economic profits differ from accounting profits in two important ways. First, they always include implicit costs, while accounting profits often do not. Second, they never include fixed costs, while accounting profits frequently do. The rationale for these differences is that economic profits focus on opportunity costs, while accounting profits do not. Because of this emphasis on opportunity costs—a central principle in economics—the term profits in this book will refer to economic profits unless noted otherwise.

8. Due to the new job opportunity offering $10 per hour, Dmitri now feels that he must earn an implicit wage of $7 per hour rather than $2 per hour. The total variable cost of each production option therefore increases by $40, i.e., 8 hours of Dmitri's time multiplied by $5 per hour ($7 minus $2). Accordingly, if Dmitri's profit in the previous situations exceeded $40 per shift, he should continue to operate his bakery; if it did not, he should close the bakery and take the alternative position.

In the initial situation Dmitri's per shift profit is $15.02. The increase in the price of gingerbread people raises his profit to $78.50; the rise in macaroon prices increases his profit to $46.84; and the rise in both prices increases his profit to $80.42. Therefore, only in the initial situation should Dmitri accept the alternative job and shut down his bakery. In the other three instances he should continue to operate as he did before.

This case illustrates the significance of work satisfaction—often a critical factor in production and employment decisions. Dmitri feels that working in his own bakery as opposed to the other bakery is worth $3 per hour to him. Without this $3 adjustment for work satisfaction, Dmitri would take the new position not only in the initial situation, but also in the situation where only macaroon prices increase.

9. The revenue and cost considerations in this situation are summarized in Table 4-6. The total revenue of each production option is the same here as in Question 6, since the cookie prices are identical in the two situations. However, since the wage of bakers' assistants during the morning shift has increased by $2 per hour, the total variable cost of those production options using one or two bakers' assistants is now higher. Specifically, the cost of those options using one assistant is now $16 higher than before, while the cost of that option using two assistants is now $32 higher.

As indicated in the table, Dmitri's profit-maximizing option is now A, which means that he will produce 23 batches of macaroons using no bakers' assistants. His profit will be $69.84.

Table 4-6

Increase in Labor Prices

Production Option	Total Revenue	Total Variable Cost	Short-Run Profit
A	$115.00	$ 45.16	$69.84
B	110.00	42.98	67.02
C	85.00	35.96	49.04
D	80.00	33.60	46.40
E	120.00	110.44	9.56
F	145.00	113.86	31.14
G	185.00	120.58	64.42
H	180.00	117.50	62.50
L	240.00	193.98	46.02

As indicated above, this situation is the same as that discussed in Question 6 except for the increase in the price of labor. What are the results of this increase? First, Dmitri shifts away from the now higher-priced input and decreases his employment of bakers' assistants from one to none. Second, he shifts his output mix toward the production of macaroons, the less labor-intensive cookie. Earlier he produced both macaroons and gingerbread people (8 batches and 29 batches respectively); now he produces only macaroons (23 batches). Third, his profit is now lower, equalling $69.84 compared to $80.42 previously. However, this decline in his profit of $10.58 is less than $16.00, the increase in the per shift wage of the single bakers' assistant employed earlier. The reason is that Dmitri diminishes the reduction in his profit by decreasing his use of labor and shifting away from the production of the more labor-intensive cookie.

This case points up once again the importance of changes in the output mix. If Dmitri were committed to producing macaroons and gingerbread people in fixed proportions, he could not substitute labor (bakers' assistants) and capital (oven) for each other to the same extent. This point holds generally. The larger the number of potential products, the greater the substitutability among inputs.

10. Dmitri clearly meets both definitions, and he is thus an entrepreneur. An important dimension of being an entrepreneur is implicit rather than explicit in these definitions. The entrepreneur is an active decision maker. He or she frequently assesses the environment, searching for changes that may require action. The entrepreneur then evaluates the changes and takes action based upon such evaluation. Dmitri exemplifies these points. If an output or input price changes, he does not remain passive. Instead, he evaluates the new situation and takes appropriate action, whether that be modifying his output mix, changing his use of inputs, or both.

Important Concepts

Perfect Competition

Long Run

Multitudes of Buyers and Sellers

Freedom of Entry and Exit

Product Homogeneity

Widespread Knowledge

Elasticity of Supply

Constant-cost Industry

Marginal Cost

Average Cost

Economic Profit

Returns to Scale

Economies of Volume

Constant Returns to Scale

Net Benefit to Community

Consumer Surplus

Horizontal Summation of Supply

Market Supply Curve

Market Demand Curve

Increasing-cost Industry

Decreasing-cost Industry

5

Taxis in Abundance
The Smooth Complexity
of Perfect Competition

The curtain rises on the hypothetical Texas metropolis of San Cristobal. It is early morning, a workday, and the hazy sun shines down on the city's one million inhabitants. Rush hour is in full swing. Sidewalks are filling with people busily making their way among their fellow pedestrians. The streets are already dense with rushing, honking vehicles, among them our main characters: the taxicab fleet of San Cristobal.

The elements of the plot are as follows:

- With few exceptions, the city's many taxicabs are owned by their drivers. No one person owns more than seven cabs, and all owners are profit maximizers.
- The only governmental restriction on either owning or driving a cab is that the driver must possess a valid state driver's license. Taxicab fares are not regulated by the city or by any other governmental entity.
- There is a large pool of potential drivers available at $20 per four-hour shift. Drivers can be hired for one, two, or three shifts per day, but they cannot be hired for periods of time less than one shift. Potential drivers, including owners, have other work opportunities which are readily available and which pay $5 per hour.
- The nonlabor costs of operating a cab, including gasoline, oil, tire, and repair expenses are $.25 per mile.
- Taxicabs currently in service depreciate at the rate of $4,380 per year. Although it may take several weeks, potential or present cab owners can buy new taxicabs in a large regional market at a constant price, such that newly purchased cabs will also depreciate at the rate of $4,380 per year. Further, there is an active regional market for

used cabs. Its presence permits cab owners to sell their vehicles at prices which reflect the yearly depreciation rate of $4,380, although again it may require several weeks to successfully complete a transaction.

- The average trip in San Cristobal consists of the following: a one-mile, three-minute drive to one of the city's numerous cab stands; a waiting time of ten minutes for the cab to work its way through the queue of other taxicabs and/or wait for passengers to arrive; a one-minute period to load passengers; a five-mile, fourteen-minute drive to the passenger's destination; and finally, a two-minute period during which the fare is paid and the passengers are discharged.
- If a taxicab operates in this Texas city, it makes eight trips per shift, and it works five four-hour shifts per day, seven day per week. Unless the cab is withdrawn from the taxi industry and sold, it operates fifty-two weeks per year.
- Services provided by different cabs and drivers are essentially identical and there is no distinction among them in the eyes of consumers.
- In San Cristobal, taxicab owners and consumers have widespread knowledge of each other's actions.

1. Is the San Cristobal taxi industry characterized by perfect competition?

2. Kristine Kirkpatrick owns two taxicabs in San Cristobal. She drives one or the other cab 44 to 50 hours per week, and employs drivers for the remaining time. Is Kristine's firm characterized by increasing, constant, or decreasing returns to scale?

3. The long run is defined as the time frame in which all inputs required by the firm are variable. What is Kristine's marginal cost per trip and her average cost per trip in the long run?

4. Is the taxi industry in San Cristobal an increasing-cost, constant-cost, or decreasing-cost industry?

5. If the fare is $5.00 per trip, will potential cab owners enter the San Cristobal taxi industry or will existing cab owners leave? Which of these actions will occur if the price is $4.00 per trip? Which if the fare is $4.30 per trip?

6. Consumers in San Cristobal demand taxicab services, not taxicabs. However, since each taxicab makes eight trips per shift and operates five shifts per day, the market demand for taxicab services can be transformed into the market demand for taxicabs. The latter is shown below.

$$Q = 1,200 - 150P$$

Where Q = number of taxicabs in San Cristobal; and
$\quad\quad P$ = price per trip.

Plot this market demand curve in Figure 5–1. Based upon responses to previous questions, what is the shape of the long-run supply curve? Plot this curve in the figure. At long-run equilibrium in the taxi industry, what will be the price per trip, the number of cabs, and the total number of cab trips per day?

Figure 5-1

Long-run Equilibrium in the Taxi Industry

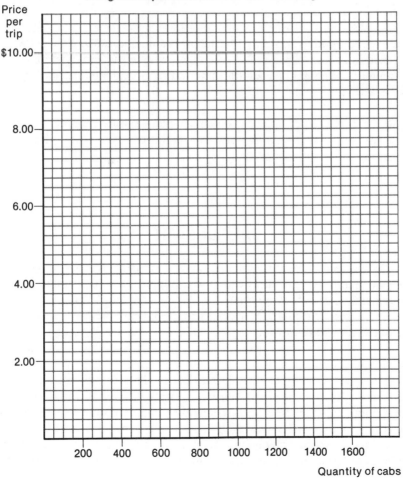

7. Based on the shapes of the demand and supply curves in Figure 5–1, do some consumers value taxi services more than others? Are some producers able to provide taxi services at a lower cost than others?

8. Assume for the moment that there are no taxicabs in San Cristobal. How much would the public be willing to pay per day to have the services of one taxicab? That is, what amount of other goods and services (measured in dollars per day) would consumers be willing to sacrifice for the services of this taxicab?

What will be the cost per day of providing the services of one taxicab? That is, what amount of other goods and services (measured in dollars per day) would the community of San Cristobal have to give up in order to have one taxicab? What is thus the net benefit or loss to the San Cristobal community that arises from having one taxicab as opposed to none?

9. Based upon the responses to the preceding questions, what is the net benefit or loss, expressed in dollars per day, to the San Cristobal community of having the equilibrium number of taxicabs as compared to no taxicabs?

10. Actual and potential cab owners in San Cristobal are identical in terms of the production of taxi services. Is this characteristic a necessary condition of perfect competition?

DISCUSSION

1. Perfect competition exists in an industry if four conditions prevail. First, there must be many producers and consumers. As a consequence, each is small relative to the market, so that each is a price taker. Second, actual and potential producers must be free to enter and leave the industry. Consumers must have similar freedom of entry and exit, although barriers to consumer entry are much less common than barriers to producer entry.

Third, there must be product homogeneity. To meet this condition, the products of the industry need not be precisely the same from a technical standpoint, but they must be sufficiently similar that consumers do not detect significant differences among them. Fourth, both consumers and producers must be knowledgeable about occurrences in the industry. This condition is sometimes termed the perfect information requirement.

While not incorrect, this term may be deceptive since it may imply that producers and consumers have knowledge about future events. Such foresight is not necessary for perfect competition. All that is required is that there be widespread knowledge among producers and consumers about current activities in the industry.

The San Cristobal taxi industry meets all four of these conditions. There are many taxicabs as well as many consumers; actual and potential taxicab owners are free to enter or leave the industry (as are consumers); taxicab services are essentially identical; and widespread knowledge exists. Perfect competition therefore characterizes the taxi industry in this Texas city.

2. The law of diminishing returns examines the results of increasing one input when at least one other input is held constant. In contrast, the principle of returns to scale focuses on what happens when the firm's inputs are increased or decreased proportionately. For example, if the firm's inputs are doubled, does output more than double, precisely double, or less than double? If the first, increasing returns to scale exist; if the second, constant returns to scale are present; if the third, decreasing returns to scale prevail.

Any cab operating in San Cristobal makes eight trips per shift and works five shifts per day. It therefore makes 40 trips per day. The daily output of Kristine's two cabs is thus 80 trips.

The output of Kristine's cabs does not depend on who is driving them. As a driver Kristine is neither more nor less proficient than those she hires. Further, if Kristine were to purchase two additional cabs, she would be able to employ proficient drivers to operate them. Similarly, Kristine could obtain for the new cabs nonlabor inputs whose quality would be identical to that of the nonlabor inputs that she now uses. The two new cabs would thus operate in the same way as the two existing ones. The combined daily output of the four cabs would therefore be 160 trips, or precisely double the current output of 80 trips.

Kristine's firm is thus characterized by constant returns to scale. The same is true for all firms in the San Cristobal taxi industry. That is, if any firm doubles or triples its inputs, its output will double or triple. Similarly, if any firm halves its inputs, its output will fall by 50 percent.

Returns to scale is a useful concept, but it has a serious weakness. It calls for all of the firm's inputs to increase in the same proportion. Often this is impossible, or if not impossible, inefficient. Further, analysis of returns to scale frequently bogs down in definitional issues. For example, does doubling of a firm's labor inputs mean that each type of labor input must be doubled, that total employment must be doubled, or that payroll must be doubled?

Because of these difficulties, a less restrictive concept is often more valuable than the concept of returns to scale. This concept will be termed economies of volume in this book; it is defined in the following way. Economies of volume will be said to exist if average cost falls as output increases in the situation where the firm is free to vary all inputs and where all input prices remain unchanged. Conversely, diseconomies of volume will be deemed present if average cost rises as output increases in this situation.

3. Since all inputs are variable in the long run, all costs are also variable, Kristine incurs three types of costs in operating a cab in San Cristobal. First, there are the nonlabor operating costs which equal $.25 per mile. Since the average trip entails a six-mile drive (five miles with the passenger and one mile to the cab stand), nonlabor operating costs per trip equal $1.50.

Second, there are the labor costs of operating a cab. These costs are the same whether Kristine drives the cab or hires someone else for this task. This is so since both owners and other potential drivers have readily available work opportunities outside the taxi industry which pay $5 per hour. The opportunity cost of driving a cab is therefore $5 per hour, and owners must pay drivers a wage equal to this amount, either explicitly to others or implicitly to themselves. Since each cab operates 20 hours per day, the cost of driver labor per day is $100 (20 hours times $5 per hour), or $2.50 per trip ($100 per day divided by 40 trips per day).

The third type of cost arises because of the depreciation of the cab. Cabs depreciate at the rate of $4,380 per year. Since Kristine's cabs work every day of the year, the daily depreciation cost is $12 ($4,380 divided by 365 days). The per trip depreciation expense is thus $.30 ($12 per day divided by 40 trips per day).

Kristine's marginal cost per trip in the long run is the sum of these three components. It therefore equals $4.30 per trip, i.e., $1.50 in nonlabor operating costs, $2.50 in labor operating costs, and $.30 in depreciation.

Kristine's marginal cost is the same for both cabs and for all trips made by the cabs. That being the case, average cost must equal marginal cost. Hence, Kristine's average cost in the long run is also $4.30 per trip.

4. Current and potential owners can readily enter and leave the taxi industry in the Texas city. Both present owners and new entrants face the same cost schedules. Each owner's marginal cost in the long run is thus the same as Kristine's, i.e., $4.30 per trip. The long-run marginal cost of providing taxi service in San Cristobal is therefore independent of the number of trips taken. The marginal cost of providing the 100th trip is $4.30 as is the marginal cost of providing the 1,000th or 10,000th trip. The same is true for long-run average cost. It equals $4.30 regardless of the number of trips taken in the Texas city.

The San Cristobal taxi industry is thus a constant-cost industry. If long-run marginal and average costs were to rise as output increased, the industry would be an increasing-cost industry. Conversely, if these costs were to fall as output decreased, the industry would be a decreasing-cost industry.

5. As discussed above, the long-run marginal cost of operating a cab in San Cristobal is $4.30 per trip. If the price is $5.00 per trip, potential owners can make an economic profit of $.70 per trip by entering the taxicab industry. Since each cab makes 40 trips per day, potential owners can thus make $28 more per day in the taxi industry than in alternative pursuits. They will therefore enter the industry. Similarly, current owners may purchase and then operate additional cabs. This process will continue until the price is driven downward to the long-run marginal cost of $4.30 per trip.

The converse holds if the price is $4.00 per trip. In this situation the economic profit of current owners is negative, equalling −$.30 per trip. Hence, present owners will either leave the industry entirely or will reduce the number of cabs that they are operating. This departure from the industry will continue until the fare is driven upward to $4.30, the long-run marginal cost per trip.

If the fare is $4.30 per trip, price equals long-run marginal cost. There will therefore be no incentive for current owners to leave the taxi industry or for potential owners to enter.

6. The market demand curve can be plotted directly from its equation, which indicates that quantity is a linear function of price. That is, the demand curve is a straight line. Accordingly, to draw the demand curve it is only necessary to determine two points on the curve. When P equals zero, Q equals 1,200 cabs; when Q equals zero, P equals $8 per trip. The market demand curve is thus a straight line which intersects the price axis at a price of $8 and the quantity axis at a quantity of 1,200 cabs. It is depicted in Figure 5−2.

In any industry the long-run supply curve for the industry is calculated by horizontally summing the long-run supply curves of the actual or potential producers in the industry. That is, to determine the output all producers are willing to offer at a given price, it is necessary to add up the individual outputs of those producers whose marginal costs are less than or equal to the price. Although complicated in some instances, this technique is straightforward for the San Cristobal taxi industry. For

69

Figure 5-2

Long-run Equilibrium in the Taxi Industry

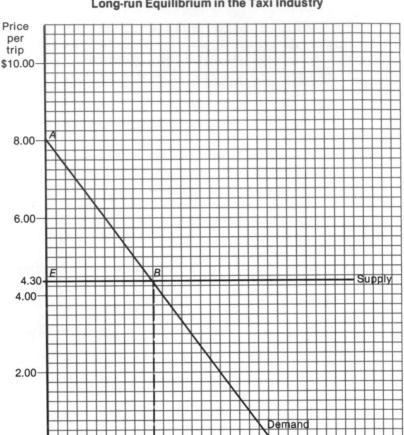

both current producers and potential entrants, long-run marginal cost is constant at $4.30 per trip. The long-run supply curve is therefore perfectly elastic at that price. It is shown graphically in Figure 5–2.

This result holds for any constant-cost industry. That is, in such an industry the long-run supply curve will be perfectly elastic. In contrast, in an increasing-cost industry the long-run supply curve will be upward sloping, while in a decreasing-cost industry it will be downward sloping.

The long-run equilibrium price is determined by the perfectly elastic supply curve. It therefore equals $4.30 per trip. Since the equilibrium price equals $4.30 per trip, the number of taxicabs can be determined by inserting this value into the demand equation. Proceeding in this way, the long-run equilibrium quantity of cabs is 555, i.e., 1200 minus 150 times $4.30, which in turn equals 1,200 minus 645. Since each cab makes 40 trips per day, the total number of daily trips is 22,200 at long-run equilibrium.

7. The long-run demand curve in the San Cristobal taxi industry is downward sloping. This means that some consumers value taxi services more than others. Illustrating this point, the services of the first cab are valued at $8.00 per trip, while those of the 555th cab arc valued at $4.30 per trip. That is to say, certain consumers are willing to pay $8.00 for a cab trip, while other consumers are only willing to pay $4.30. San Cristobal consumers are thus not identical in terms of the demand for taxi services.

As discussed before, all actual or potential taxi owners face the same cost schedules. It is this factor which makes long-run marginal cost constant at $4.30 per trip. Put another way, it means that no owner can produce taxi services at a cost lower than those of other owners. Unlike consumers, actual and potential owners are thus identical in terms of the production of taxi services.

8. As described above, consumers are willing to pay approximately $8 per trip for the services of the first cab. Since this cab would make 40 trips per day, consumers would be willing to pay $320 per day for the services of the cab. That is, the daily value that consumers place on such services is $320.

The cost of these services to the community is the long-run marginal cost of $4.30 per trip multiplied by 40 trips per day, or $172 per day. The difference between the value that consumers place on a set of services and the cost of those services to the community is the net benefit or loss of those services to the community. Therefore, in this instance the net benefit to the community from having one taxicab, as opposed to none, is $148 per day.

9. As discussed in the responses to the previous questions, the value that consumers place on taxi services is shown by the demand curve. Accordingly, the value to consumers and thus to the San Cristobal community of having the services of 555 cabs, rather than no cabs, is the area under the demand curve up to the quantity of 555 cabs, i.e., the area of the trapezoid *ABCD* in Figure 5–2. Similarly, the cost to the community of having 555 cabs as opposed to none is the area under the supply curve up to the quantity of 555 cabs, i.e., the area of the rectangle *EBCD* in Figure 5–2

The net benefit to the San Cristobal community of having 555 cabs, rather than no cabs, is the difference between the value of the services provided by this number of cabs and the costs incurred by using these cabs. The net benefit to the community therefore equals the difference between the area under the demand curve and the area under the supply curve up to the quantity of 555 cabs, i.e., the area of the right triangle *ABE* in Figure 5–2. The area of a right triangle equals one-half times one side times the other side of the triangle. In this case one side of the triangle is the 555 taxicabs and the other is the benefit to the community of the first cab, which equals $148 per day. The net benefit to the San Cristobal community of having 555 cabs as compared to none is therefore $41,070 per day, i.e., one-half times $148 per cab per day times 555 cabs.

Since the opportunity cost of providing taxicabs is constant in this case, the net benefit to the community falls entirely to the consumer of taxicab services. That is, it is consumers who reap the daily benefit of having the taxi industry in San Cristobal. The net gain by consumers is termed consumer surplus. Since in this case consumer surplus equals the net benefit to the community, it is also graphically represented by the triangle *ABE* in Figure 5–2.

10. As discussed earlier, the San Cristobal taxi industry is characterized by perfect competition since it meets the necessary four conditions: multitudes of buyers and sellers, freedom of entry and exit, product homogeneity, and widespread knowledge. However, none of these four conditions, either individually or collectively, mandates that producers be identical. This characteristic is therefore not a requirement of perfect competition. It is compatible with perfect competition, but it is not a necessary component. For example, a large agricultural market can approximate perfect competition, and producers in such a market are usually not identical. The same holds for trading in a widely held stock on a major exchange.

II

EXTENSIONS OF COMPETITIVE MARKET THEORY

Section I emphasizes basic economic analysis, concluding appropriately in Chapter 5 with an examination of a perfectly competitive industry. This section begins the process of moving closer toward reality by stripping away the assumptions of the perfectly competitive model. However, the deviations from that model are less extreme here than in later chapters.

The subject of Chapter 6 is a unique brick-oven bakery in the small town of Black Diamond, Washington. This bakery brings to mind an interesting cluster of issues. Its very existence is an apparent paradox since it is a successful firm, but there are no other brick-oven bakeries in the Puget Sound region. Similarly, if the bakery had been built in downtown Seattle or Odessa, Washington, would it have survived? The bakery's clientele is not homogeneous. How does this influence its marketing strategy?

During the last two centuries both the bread and nail industries have been markedly affected by technological change, but yet the effects have been dissimilar. Why?

In many markets there is not only a flow of newly produced goods, but also a stock of goods which are currently being used by consumers. This duality is particularly striking for houses since they remain valuable structures for many years. Chapter 7 takes as its subject the market for houses in three distinctive communities in the Denver metropolitan area. The chapter emphasizes the relationships between stocks and flows, focusing on the interplay between the market for houses and the rate of house construction. It analyzes the housing effects of four events which could and have occurred in many locales: a gasoline shortage, establishment of a major new firm, development of a new residential area, and passage of a low-growth law.

Important Concepts

Specialized Firm
Durable Input
Product Quality
Quasi-rent
Opportunity Cost
Heterogeneity of Consumers
Loss Leader
Marketing Strategy
Location Benefits
Location Costs
Technological Change
Cost-reducing Innovation
Quality-enhancing Innovation
Implicit Costs
Economic Profit
Income Elasticity of Demand

6

On the Existence
of Brick Ovens

A Study
of an Unusual Firm

The principal subject of this chapter is the Black Diamond Bakery, which is located in the small town of the same name in the Puget Sound region of Washington state. Black Diamond is situated in a rural area, approximately thirty miles from both Seattle and Tacoma. The bakery is a real firm, and its general description in this chapter is accurate. However, many of the details mentioned were developed to enhance discussion and are thus hypothetical.

The Black Diamond Bakery is famous for the quality of bread baked in its old brick oven. This oven was built in 1902 and is the only commercial wood-fired baking oven in Washington. It puts out an even, moisture-retaining heat which, according to many of the bakery's customers, makes bread moist on the inside with a thick surrounding crust.

Every day a wood fire is built inside the oven and allowed to burn for eight to ten hours. The ashes are then removed and the oven is cleaned for the day's baking. Breads are baked for approximately one hour, and the oven can accomodate about 120 loaves of any type of bread at one time. After four one-hour baking shifts the heat of the oven has dissipated to the point that its performance is no longer considered satisfactory by the bakery's proprietor. The maximum daily output of the bakery is thus about 480 loaves of bread. Aside from the daily cleaning, the oven requires little maintenance; its surface bricks need not be replaced more often than every ten years.

The bread produced by the Black Diamond Bakery is sold through a small store in the front of the bakery. This store is closed on Mondays and Tuesdays but is open from 9:00 A.M. to 6:00 P.M., or until all the bread is sold, on the other five days. In most instances the bakery is sold out by closing time on weekdays and by 4:00 P.M. or even earlier on weekends. The bakery does not advertise its products in the local media.

The great majority of the bakery's customers fall into two groups. The first is individuals who live relatively close to the bakery, i.e., perhaps within a ten-mile radius. The second is skiers, hikers, and other outdoor enthusiasts who come to the bakery at least partially because of its location: Black Diamond is situated on one of the main roads between Seattle and two recreational attractions—the Crystal Mountain ski area and Mt. Rainier National Park.

1. As noted, there are no other bakeries in the state of Washington which have brick ovens similar to the one in the Black Diamond Bakery. The Black Diamond firm makes at least a moderate profit. Why have other entrepreneurs not entered the brick-oven baking business? What factor(s) explain the apparent paradox that there is a profitable brick-oven bakery in Black Diamond but no brick-oven bakeries elsewhere in the Puget Sound region?

2. Sourdough French bread is a specialty bread which the Black Diamond Bakery sells only on Saturday. While the costs of producing this bread are relatively high, profits are also higher since the price more than compensates for the higher cost. Assuming that the bakery tries to maximize profits, should it sell sourdough bread on Wednesdays as well as on Saturdays? On Sundays as well as on Saturdays?

3. During this century the income of American consumers has steadily risen. If this trend continues, what will be the likely impact on the demand for sourdough French bread as compared to the demand for ordinary white bread?

4. A loss leader is a product deliberately sold by a retailer at a price below cost in order to attract customers to the store. Should the Black Diamond Bakery use this sales technique?

5. Seattle is the center of a large and prosperous metropolitan area. Odessa is situated in the wheat country of eastern Washington, more than fifty miles from the nearest city. It is located at the juncture of two state highways, but it is not on a major transportation route. Like Black Diamond, Odessa has approximately one thousand inhabitants.

If the bakery with its single brick oven had been built in 1902 not in Black Diamond but in downtown Seattle, would it still exist? Would it exist if it had been built in Odessa?

6. The proprietor of the Black Diamond Bakery lives in a comfortable house on a wooded lot close to Black Diamond. His neighbor is Louise Hawley, who opened a book and record store several years ago in Enumclaw, a town near Black Diamond. The sole owner of the store, Louise actively manages the business and works there on a full-time basis. She has one full-time employee and several part-time workers. During the last year her total revenues were $168,000 and her merchandise costs were $104,000. She paid her employees $19,000, including their payroll taxes. Her rent was $12,000 and her other out-of-pocket costs were $9,000. Did Louise earn an economic profit of $24,000 during the last year?

7. Two hundred years ago nails and bread were made by hand in labor-intensive processes. Today, reflecting technological change essentially all nails are mass-produced using capital-intensive techniques. In contrast, the impact of technological change on the bread industry has been different. Bread is now mass-produced in large capital-intensive bakeries, but it is also produced by smaller bakeries which use more labor-intensive techniques. What factors account for the dissimilar effects of technological change on the nail and bread industries?

DISCUSSION

1. The Black Diamond Bakery is a highly specialized firm whose chief asset is the brick oven. Built more than seventy-five years ago, this oven now requires little maintenance. Its alternative uses are severely limited, and its value as a pile of bricks is trivial. The opportunity cost of the oven thus approaches zero. As a result, the marginal costs incurred by operating the Black Diamond Bakery even over a time frame of several years include only the costs of labor and materials used to produce the bread and the alternative cost of the land upon which the bakery is situated.

In contrast, the marginal costs of an entrepreneur debating whether to enter the brick-oven bakery business include not only these costs, but also the cost of building a new brick oven. Construction of the oven is an intricate labor-intensive task, and therefore expensive. The marginal cost facing a potential entrant is thus substantially higher than the marginal cost facing the proprietor of the Black Diamond Bakery.

It is thus likely that the total revenue earned by selling the high-quality breads produced by a brick-oven bakery is not sufficient to cover the opportunity cost of setting up a new bakery, even though such revenue exceeds the opportunity cost of operating the already existing Black Diamond Bakery. That is, even in the long run the marginal revenue of brick-oven bakery operation falls intermediate between the marginal cost of operating the Black Diamond Bakery and the marginal cost of constructing and then operating a new brick-oven bakery. This being the case, the Black Diamond Bakery will continue to earn at least a moderate profit, but other firms will not enter the brick-oven bakery business since they would not find it profitable to do so.

The analysis of this question applies not only to the Black Diamond Bakery but to any firm which uses specialized durable inputs. The brick oven in the Black Diamond Bakery could as well be a forge in a steel mill or a printing press of a newspaper. The opportunity cost of these machines may be very low since their alternative uses may be limited and routine maintenance may be minimal. In such instances the equipment should be used as long as the total revenue earned by doing so exceeds the opportunity cost.

This return to a specialized durable input is termed a quasi-rent. It equals the difference between the revenue earned by the input and the opportunity cost of using it. As in the Black Diamond case, the former equals the total revenue gained by selling the final product minus the costs of the variable inputs.

2. As is true of many firms, the clientele of the Black Diamond Bakery is heterogeneous. That is, the consumers of the bakery's products are not identical. Further, they can be divided into distinctive groups whose characteristics are quite different. This being the case, in devising a marketing strategy it is essential to consider these groups and their characteristics.

One segment of the bakery's customers consists of individuals who live relatively near the bakery (who will be termed locals); and the other segment is composed of skiers, hikers, campers, etc., most of whom reside in the urban sections of metropolitan Seattle (who will be termed Seattleites). It is likely that on weekends Seattleites account for the majority of the bakery's sales, with the reverse being true on weekdays. At a minimum, given prevailing recreational patterns in this country, the ratio of Seattleites to locals among the bakery's customers will be greater on weekends than on weekdays.

It is possible and perhaps likely, but by no means certain, that these two groups of consumers have quite dissimilar tastes. In particular, Seattleites may have a much stronger preference for sourdough French bread than do locals. If this were the case, the bakery should sell sourdough bread on Sundays as well as on Saturdays, but should not offer the bread on Wednesdays. If instead the tastes of these two groups are similar, the bakery should sell sourdough bread not only on weekends but also on Wednesdays, and perhaps on Thursdays and Fridays as well (assuming that the necessary ingredients are readily available).

A further point is that it is possible that by offering the sourdough bread on additional days the bakery will reduce Saturday sales. This possibility seems unlikely for Sunday sales since the great majority of Seattleite customers probably do not make purchases at the bakery on both weekend days. That is, the Saturday and Sunday markets are largely independent. However, if sourdough bread were sold throughout the bakery's work week, local demand for the product could well be saturated. Therefore, even if the preferences of locals and Seattleites for sourdough bread are similar, the bakery may find that the most profitable option is to sell this bread only on weekends and one weekday, rather than on all five days that it is open.

3. The income elasticity of demand is analogous to the price elasticity of demand. Accordingly, it is defined as the percentage change in the quantity demanded of a product in response to a given percentage change in consumers' income. The demand for specialized high-quality breads like sourdough French is likely to be highly income elastic. In contrast, the demand for ordinary white bread is not strongly income elastic. In fact, ordinary white bread may be an inferior good. That is, as consumers' income rises, their demand for this product falls.

In any event sourdough French bread almost certainly has a higher income elasticity than does ordinary white bread. Therefore, if the upward trend in real income continues, the demand for sourdough bread will increase more than will the demand for ordinary white bread.

4. The Black Diamond Bakery now sells essentially all of its products without using loss leaders or even advertising in the local media. If the bakery employed loss leaders, it would not be able to make up its losses on the loss leader by increasing sales of other products. Its profits would thus decline, and it should therefore not use this sales technique.

The loss leader can be an important element in an effective marketing strategy, but except in unusual cases two requirements must be met for this technique to be successful. First, the store's potential customers must be numerous compared to its routine clientele. That is, the number of consumers who may or may not shop at the store must be much larger than the number that shop there regardless. Second, the store must offer a wide range of products. If it does not, the store will not gain sufficiently once customers are attracted to its premises. Given these two requirements, the loss leader technique is most effectively practiced by large stores in large markets.

5. Like other characteristics, location confers benefits and costs. Location is particularly important to the Black Diamond Bakery since the brick oven cannot be moved. In its present location the Black Diamond Bakery benefits markedly because it is situated on an important recreational route in western Washington. Its location on this route substantially increases the demand for its specialized high-quality products. Since the Black Diamond area is largely rural, the price of land is relatively low. The opportunity cost of the Black Diamond Bakery's land is therefore small.

The location of the Black Diamond Bakery thus bestows major benefits and minor costs. Location is therefore an important factor contributing to the bakery's continued existence. It is true that the Black Diamond Bakery could have survived in many other locations, but it is also true that it would have perished in many others.

Illustrating the latter point, the bakery with its single brick oven would not have survived if it had been built in either downtown Seattle or Odessa. The price of land is very high in downtown Seattle. As a consequence, the opportunity cost of the bakery's land would overwhelm its revenues. It would therefore be prudent for the bakery's owner to demolish the bakery and sell the land for alternative uses.

The difficulty facing a brick-oven bakery in Odessa would not be the high cost of land, but rather the much smaller demand for the bakery's specialized products. Although Odessa and Black Diamond have the same number of residents, Black Diamond is situated on a major travel route, while Odessa is not. As a result, the bakery's clientele in Odessa would be almost entirely limited to the inhabitants of the area. In all likelihood this population base would not be sufficient to support the brick-oven bakery. At a minimum its owner would reap much lower gains in Odessa than in Black Diamond.

6. Like Dmitri in Chapter 4, Louise is an entrepreneur. As such, she earns the difference between her total revenues and her total payments to other individuals. This difference does equal $24,000, but the entire difference is not economic profit. In fact, none of it may be economic profit.

Not included in the $144,000 of expenses are Louise's implicit costs. The largest such cost is the cost of Louise's time. Depending upon her opportunities elsewhere, this cost may be much lower than $24,000 or it may exceed that figure. To open the store Louise had to invest capital in the enterprise. The opportunity cost of this capital is another significant implicit cost. In addition, depending upon how the store operates, there may be other implicit costs.

Economic profit equals the difference between total revenues and all costs evaluated at their next best opportunity. The latter include not only Louise's payments to others, but also her implicit costs, which are substantial. Her economic profit is therefore much less than $24,000.

7. When evaluating a technological change, it is necessary to consider both its impact on product cost and its effect on product quality. If an innovation is both cost-reducing and quality-enhancing, it will be widely accepted and alternative technologies will eventually be abandoned. If an innovation is neither, no one will adopt it since it is inferior to existing technologies. Intermediate results arise when an innovation is cost-reducing but also quality-reducing, or when an innovation is quality-enhancing but also cost-increasing.

The development of capital-intensive techniques for making nails dramatically lowered the costs of production. On the whole, it also improved the quality of the final product. This innovation was thus both cost-reducing and quality-enhancing. It therefore made labor-intensive techniques for producing nails economically unfeasible. As a result, the capital-intensive technique was universally accepted and the labor-intensive technique was no longer used.

Similar results did not occur in the bread industry. Here the capital-intensive techniques lowered the cost of production, but it also reduced or at a minimum changed the quality of the final product. As a consequence, the capital-intensive technique did not make the more labor-intensive processes economically unfeasible. The latter were therefore not driven from the marketplace by the former.

Capital-intensive production of nails is thus an innovation superior on both counts, i.e., it reduces costs and improves quality. In contrast, capital-intensive production of bread is an innovation superior on one count but inferior on the other, i.e., it lowers cost but also reduces quality. That being the case, both capital-intensive and labor-intensive methods of production will coexist in the bread industry since some consumers are willing to pay a higher price for a higher quality bread, while others prefer a lower price for a lower quality bread.

Important Concepts

Interaction of Stocks and Flows
Durable Good
Stock of Houses
Rate of Net House Construction
Elasticity of Supply
Elasticity of Demand
Substitute
Price Effect
Quantity Effect
Transportation Costs
Substitution Effect
Income Effect
Government Intervention
Low-growth Law
Quota
Primary Effect
Secondary Effect

7

Changing Price of Shelter

Interaction of Stocks and Flows

An eastern outcropping of the Rocky Mountains—the striking Flat-
irons—arises abruptly from the western edge of Boulder, Colorado,
within which lies the main campus of Colorado University. A solid plu-
rality of Boulder residents are connected in one way or another with
the university. Increasingly during recent years a number of business
firms have settled in Boulder or have established branches there, especially those with a heavy research or recreational content. An expressway
connects Boulder with Denver, making it possible to traverse the twenty-
five-mile distance between the two cities in approximately 30 minutes. As
a partial consequence, a number of people live in Boulder but work in
Denver. Although located within the Denver metropolitan area, Boulder
is not a traditional suburb, but rather a small city which maintains its
own individual flavor. It contains a number of shops, restaurants, and
other service establishments.

Evergreen, Colorado is the center of a mountain community west of
Denver, which is home for at least part of the year to several well-known
singers, television personalities, and other luminaries. While within the
Denver metropolitan area, Evergreen is located in the high foothills of
the Rocky Mountains at an altitude of about seven thousand feet.
Although not a bedroom community in the classic sense, Evergreen's
business firms are largely limited to real estate companies, shops, and
other service establishments. Most of its residents work in Denver or in
the suburbs close to Denver. There are two main routes between Evergreen and Denver. Neither route is exclusively over an expressway; both
entail a travel time of 30 to 45 minutes. An hour is required to travel
between Evergreen and Boulder. The route is circuitous and can be
hazardous in inclement weather.

Cherry Creek is a loosely defined section of southeast Denver. While located within the city itself, Cherry Creek is largely residential and contains a number of elegant homes. It has no heavy industry, but it does contain many office buildings and shops. Cherry Creek is also one of Denver's entertainment centers, featuring theaters, discotheques, and restaurants. Downtown Denver is less than five miles away and can be reached in 10 to 15 minutes via a number of routes. Travel from Cherry Creek to Boulder or Evergreen consumes 45 to 50 minutes.

During the last decade Boulder, Evergreen, and Cherry Creek experienced rapid growth. Still, each community is small compared to the Denver metropolitan area. None of the three communities has more than 100,000 residents, whereas the population of the entire Denver area approximates 1.5 million. While Boulder, Evergreen, and Cherry Creek all house a diversity of people, the dominant socioeconomic status of each community is upper/middle class. The locations of the three communities within the Denver area are displayed in Figure 7–1. The primary mode of transportation in the Denver area has been and remains the automobile.

The events described in the questions below have a solid basis in fact, but to expedite discussion they are presented in simplified terms.

1. The gasoline shortage which emerged in the 1970s becomes increasingly worse. Gasoline is now selling at significantly more than $1 per gallon. It is usually available during the week and to a lesser extent on weekends, although spot shortages do occur.

What will be the impact of the gasoline shortage on the following variables over a two-year period?
- price of houses in Boulder;
- price of houses in Evergreen;
- price of houses in Cherry Creek;
- quantity of houses in Boulder;
- quantity of houses in Evergreen;
- quantity of houses in Cherry Creek;
- rate of net house construction (rate of house construction minus rate of house destruction) in Boulder;
- rate of net house construction in Evergreen;
- rate of net house construction in Cherry Creek.

2. Several years ago a large national firm decided to set up a major research laboratory in the Boulder area. This laboratory is scheduled to begin full-time operations in the next month. Upon doing so it will become one of the largest employers in the Boulder area.

What will be the impact of the new laboratory on the variables specified in Question 1 during a two-year period?

Figure 7-1

Sketch of Denver Area

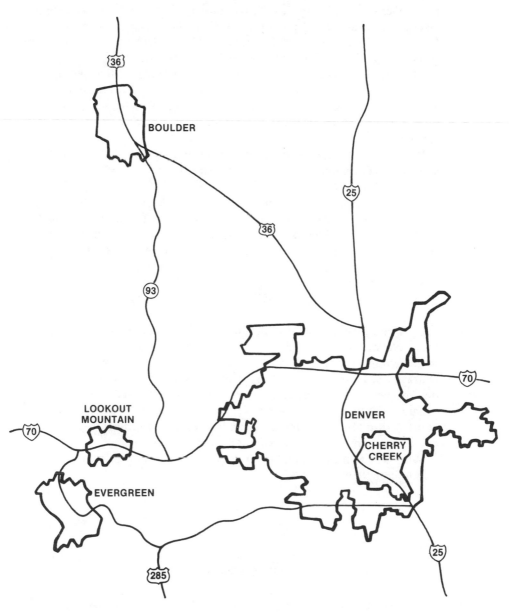

3. Genesee is a new residential development which features expensive mountain-style homes. Located in the foothills west of Denver on Lookout Mountain (shown in Figure 7–1), it has been in the planning process for five years. Genesee is adjacent to one of the two routes between Denver and Evergreen. Travel along this route from Genesee to Evergreen consumes 20 minutes; travel in the opposite direction from Genesee to Denver requires 25 minutes. Cherry Creek and Boulder are respectively 30 and 40 minutes away from Genesee.

The upcoming months are expected to be a period of intense activity in Genesee. New houses are nearing completion for sale to the public. Lots have been purchased by prospective homeowners who are having houses built to their specifications. Other lots are being offered for sale for the first time.

What will be the impact of Genesee's development on the variables specified in Question 1 over a two-year period?

4. After long and at times bitter debate, the people of Boulder pass a new law, effective in one month, which sharply limits the future growth of the community. This law places a strict ceiling on the net increase in the number of houses in the Boulder market each year. This ceiling is far below the current net rate of house construction in the Boulder area.

What will be the impact of the new law on the variables specified in Question 1 over a two-year period?

5. A new carefully planned development undertaken by Horatio Clark was underway at the time the low-growth law was passed in Boulder. It is situated in a particularly picturesque area which has distinctly different characteristics. Initially twenty-five houses were projected for Horatio's development. Ten of these houses were almost completed when the law became effective, and thus were excluded from the law's quota. The construction of the remaining fifteen houses will be subject to the law, and at a minimum will be substantially stretched out.

What will be the impact of the low-growth law on the prices of the almost completed houses?

DISCUSSION

1. Houses are durable goods which can be used for many years. In fact, if the quality of construction is good and if maintenance is routinely performed, a house may be in excellent shape even after fifty or one hundred years. Many months are usually consumed between the initial design and completion of a new house. Similarly, although an individual house can be demolished quickly, the deterioration and destruction of houses across a large market is a gradual process which cannot be accelerated easily.

The net result of these factors, especially the long life of houses, is that the stock of houses (i.e., the existing number of houses) is large compared to the net flow of new houses (i.e., the annual rate of net house construction), which is defined as the rate of house construction minus the rate of house destruction. This characteristic dominates the house market and distinguishes that market from most others. For example, like other services, the taxi services in Chapter 5 cannot be stored. They are produced and consumed during a specified time period. There is thus no stock of taxi services. As a further example, take the orange market in Chapter 2. Oranges can be inventoried, but unlike houses they cannot be used while they are being stored.

The large stock of houses compared to the net flow of new houses makes the supply curve of houses highly inelastic over a two-year time period. It is not completely inelastic since the net rate of house construction is not minute compared to the stock of houses and since that rate does vary with the price of houses. The inelasticity of supply means that any change in the demand for houses will primarily affect the price of houses, rather than the quantity of houses. However, the change in house prices will influence the rate of house construction, which will in turn affect the supply of houses, but only after a period of some years. Thus, across a long time horizon (e.g., a decade) a change in demand will influence the quantity of houses as well as the price of houses, but in shorter time periods such as two years the price effect will dominate the quantity effect.

In Boulder, Evergreen, and Cherry Creek the demand for houses will be elastic since there are ready substitutes available, ranging from apartments to houses elsewhere in metropolitan Denver. However, each community has distinctive characteristics and thus the demand for houses in each will not be fully elastic.

In the three communities the supply of new house construction will be elastic, but not completely so. On the one hand, many productive resources, including labor and capital equipment, can swing back and forth between house construction and other forms of construction. On the other hand, some of these resources are more skilled at building houses than are others. Further, the nonuniformity of land in the three communities contributes to the upward-sloping nature of the supply curve for house construction.

The impact of the gasoline shortage clearly illustrates these general principles. The sharp rise in gasoline prices and the decline in its availability will reduce the demand for houses in Boulder. However, the effect will be circumscribed since many Boulder residents work in the community and are thus less affected by the gasoline shortage. The Boulder situation is portrayed in Figures 7−2 and 7−3. In the former the demand for houses decreases modestly from D_0 to D_1. Because the supply of houses, S_0, is highly inelastic, the change in demand produces a very small decline in the quantity of houses and a larger but still modest decrease in the price of houses.

Both the demand and supply curves in Figure 7−2 reflect expectations about what will occur during the two-year period in addition to the gasoline shortage. Accordingly, the small decline in the quantity of houses should not be interpreted as an absolute decrease, but rather as

Figure 7-2

Impact of Gasoline Shortage: Boulder House Market

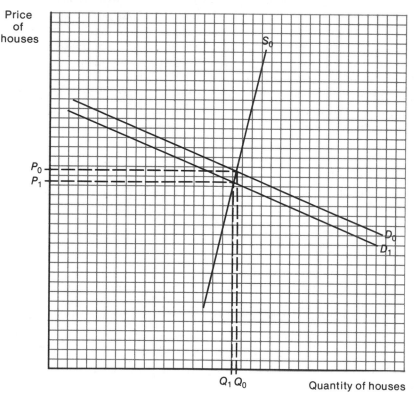

a decrease compared to what would have been the case at the end of two years in the absence of the gasoline shortage. The price decrease should be interpreted in a similar manner. This principle holds throughout this chapter.

As indicated in Figure 7–3, the modest decrease in Boulder house prices exerts a proportionately larger effect on the rate of house construction, because the supply curve for the latter is relatively elastic. The gasoline shortage thus induces an appreciable fall in the net rate of Boulder house construction from C_0 to C_1.

The impact of the gasoline shortage on the Evergreen house market is similar, but much stronger. A high percentage of Evergreen residents work in Denver and commute back and forth each day. The increase in their transportation costs will be substantial. Prospective house buyers must also consider the rise in transportation costs.

Figure 7-3

Impact of Gasoline Shortage: Boulder House Construction

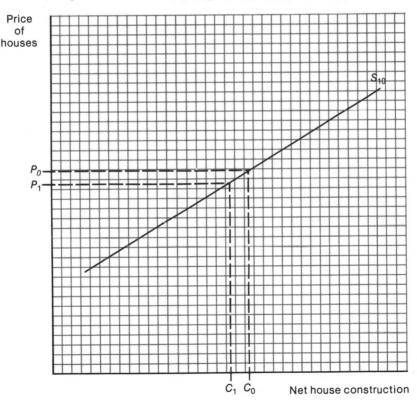

The increased transportation costs will have two effects. First, they will make it relatively more expensive to live in Evergreen than in areas closer to Denver. Consumers will therefore substitute toward the latter and away from the former. Second, they will decrease the real income of consumers. Both these substitution and income effects will decrease the demand for houses in Evergreen.

The Evergreen situation is depicted in Figure 7–4, where demand declines substantially from D_{20} to D_{21}. Even so, the quantity effect is small, with the number of houses decreasing from Q_{20} to Q_{21}. In contrast, the price effect is sizable, with the price of houses declining from P_{20} to P_{21}. As displayed in Figure 7–5, the decline in house prices exerts an even stronger influence on the net rate of house construction, which decreases from C_{20} to C_{21}.

The gasoline shortage has the reverse effects in the Cherry Creek area.

Figure 7-4

Impact of Gasoline Shortage: Evergreen House Market

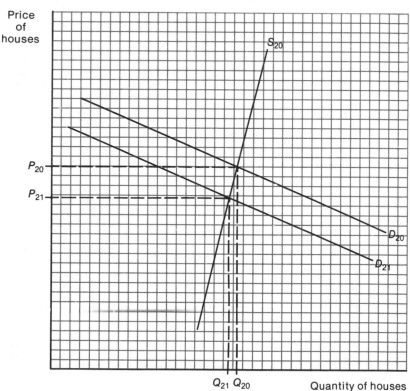

Figure 7-5

Impact of Gasoline Shortage: Evergreen House Construction

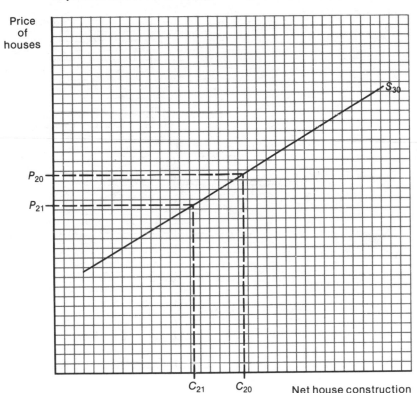

The rise in transportation costs increases the attractiveness of living in Cherry Creek as compared to living in Boulder, Evergreen, or other outlying communities. The increase in gasoline prices will decrease the real income of Cherry Creek residents, which could in turn reduce their demand for housing. However, this income effect will be smaller than the substitution effect produced by consumers shifting toward Cherry Creek and away from outlying areas.

The demand for houses will therefore increase in the Cherry Creek market. However, the magnitude of the increase here will be less than the size of the decrease in the Evergreen market, where the substitution and income effects are both strong and mutually reinforcing. As shown in Figure 7–6, the increase in the demand for houses produces a small rise in the quantity of houses and a larger increase in the price of houses. The

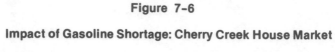

Figure 7-6

Impact of Gasoline Shortage: Cherry Creek House Market

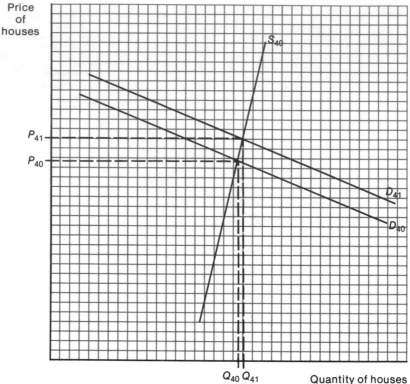

price increase in turn produces a proportionately larger increase in the net rate of house construction, as shown in Figure 7-7.

2. Some of the new staff hired by the laboratory will be current Boulder residents, but many more will be recruited from outside Boulder and outside Colorado. The latter actions alone will substantially increase the demand for houses in Boulder. Further, presuming that the new laboratory pays current Boulder residents a higher salary than they were earning previously, the former action will also increase the demand for houses, albeit not to the same extent. Recalling the inelasticity of the supply of houses, the increase in demand will produce a small rise in the quantity of houses in Boulder and a larger increase in the price of houses. The latter in turn will exert an even stronger influence on the net rate of house construction, which will therefore increase markedly in Boulder.

94

Figure 7-7

Impact of Gasoline Shortage: Cherry Creek House Construction

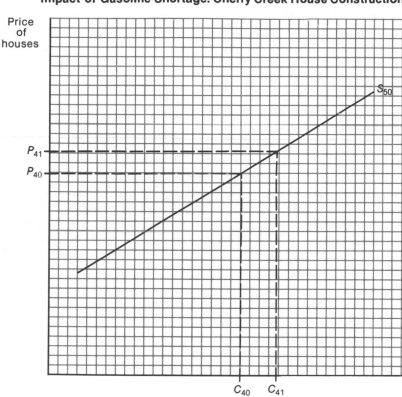

Net house construction

The primary effect of the new laboratory will be felt in the Boulder house market. While the opening of the new laboratory could have secondary effects in the Cherry Creek and Evergreen markets, such effects are unlikely to be significant because of the distances between Boulder and the other two communities. It takes 45 minutes to drive from Cherry Creek to Boulder. The trip from Evergreen to Boulder is even longer, and the route is circuitous and at times hazardous.

3. Genesee is relatively close to Evergreen. Compared to the latter, the former has the substantial advantage of being significantly closer to the city of Denver. Like Evergreen, Genesee is located in the foothills of the Rockies. The houses in Genesee are at least somewhat similar to those in Evergreen. For all these reasons, Genesee and Evergreen houses are relatively close substitutes for each other. Put in another way, suppliers of houses in Evergreen or Genesee are competing with each other to attract consumers and to then sell them houses.

The increased availability of houses (and land for houses) in Genesee will therefore decrease the demand for houses in Evergreen. As a consequence, the quantity of houses in Evergreen will decline by a small amount and the price of houses will decrease significantly more. The decline in Evergreen house prices will then result in a substantial decrease in the rate of house construction.

It is possible but unlikely that the development of Genesee will decrease to a modest extent the demand for houses in Cherry Creek. It is possible because Genesee is closer to Cherry Creek and Denver than are either Boulder or Evergreen. It is unlikely because Genesee is still 30 minutes away from Cherry Creek and because Genesee's mountain setting is markedly different from Cherry Creek's urban setting.

The opening of Genesee is even less likely to have a significant impact on the Boulder market. Although closer to Boulder than is Evergreen, Genesee is nevertheless 40 minutes away over a circuitous, potentially hazardous route.

4. The passage of the low-growth law is a form of government intervention in the marketplace. Although different in origin, it is similar in effect to the use of quotas in agricultural markets. Such quotas have long been a feature of federal government policy in this country.

By fiat the low-growth law will reduce the rate of net house construction. That is, this rate cannot exceed the ceiling specified in the law. Accordingly, above the ceiling it will no longer be responsive to the price of houses. This is illustrated in Figure 7−8, where the initial supply of net house construction is S_{10}. The postlaw supply curve, S_{11}, follows S_{10} until the ceiling specified in the law (C_1) is reached. At C_1 the new supply curve becomes perfectly inelastic since the rate of net house construction cannot exceed this limit.

The prelaw supply of houses, S_0 in Figure 7−9, shows the quantities of houses that would be offered by suppliers at different house prices at the end of the two-year period. It is based on the assumption that the rate of net house construction will respond to the price of houses in the manner depicted by S_{10} in Figure 7−8. However, this is no longer true at prices higher than P_2. The postlaw supply of houses, S_1 in Figure 7−9, is therefore perfectly inelastic at prices above P_2, with the difference between the supply curves becoming progressively greater as the price of houses increases.

Except for the sharp decline in the rate of net house construction from C_0 to C_1, the results in this situation are not striking over a two-year period. The price effect is small, with price increasing from P_0 to P_1.

Figure 7-8

Impact of Low-growth Law: Boulder House Construction

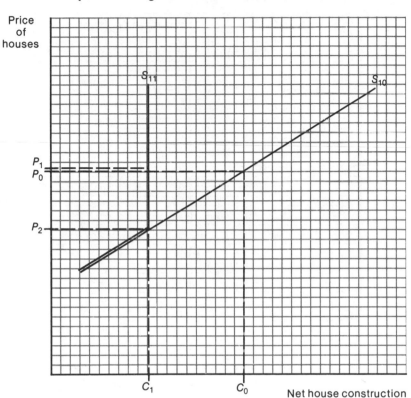

The extent of the price rise is limited by the substantial elasticity of demand. The quantity effect is also modest, as the number of houses declines from Q_0 to Q_1. The reason is that although the new supply curve is more inelastic than the initial one, the latter is still highly inelastic. The potential for change in the direction of inelasticity is thus limited.

Since the change in the price of Boulder houses is modest, it is likely once again that the secondary effects will be insignificant. That is, the new Boulder law will not have an appreciable impact on the Evergreen and Cherry Creek markets.

Over a longer time period a low-growth law may have a substantial impact on both the price and quantity of houses. For example, if the time horizon were a decade, the initial supply curve in Figure 7-9 would be much more elastic. That being the case, the difference between S_0 and S_1 would be much greater. Another point is that the passage of a low-

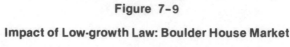

Figure 7-9

Impact of Low-growth Law: Boulder House Market

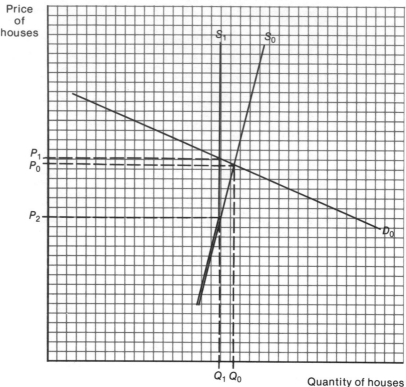

growth law implies the expectation that demand for houses will continue to be high. This expectation is built into demand curve D_0 in Figure 7–9. However, the expectation may be erroneous and demand may be even higher than was expected. If this occurs, the impact of the low-growth law will be greater than that discussed above. To examine the joint influence of a low-growth law and an increase in demand, consider the combined effects of the events described in this question and Question 2.

5. For Boulder as a whole, the influence of the low-growth law is muted by the fact that the stock of houses is large compared to the rate of net house construction. However, such a stock/flow relationship does not characterize Horatio's development. While substitutes for the development's houses undoubtedly exist in Boulder and elsewhere in the Denver metropolitan area, the development is described as being unusually picturesque with distinctive characteristics. It is therefore unlikely that the demand for its houses is completely price elastic. That being the case, since the number available in the short run will be ten or perhaps a few more rather than twenty-five as projected, the prices of the almost completed houses will increase significantly.

III

IMPERFECT COMPETITION

The model of perfect competition is useful from two perspectives. First, it serves as a foundation upon which to build other types of analyses. Second, the characteristics of some industries approximate those of perfect competition. However, the conditions of most industries do not. Some deviations from perfect competition were examined in the previous section. This section addresses other, more fundamental departures.

Chapter 8 is directed toward a classic monopoly situation—a single toll road serving an isolated village. The chapter considers whether this road is a natural monopoly, and explores the implications of this point. It analyzes in depth two alternative models for operating a moncpoly: profit maximization and welfare maximization. In doing so it addresses a range of issues. For example, will the profit maximizer or the welfare maximizer produce a higher output? Will either engage in price discrimination, and if so, under what circumstances? What considerations must the welfare maximizer take into account in devising a tax package to cover an operating deficit? In addition, this chapter considers, albeit in less detail, yet a third model for monopoly operation, i.e., average cost pricing.

Chapter 9 takes up another kind of industry which is more common in this country than either monopoly or perfect competition. The chapter's setting is the movie theater industry in a medium-sized metropolitan area; its subject is differentiated oligopoly. The chapter emphasizes the interdependence of oligopolists, which contrasts with the independence of both the monopolist and the perfect competitor. This interdependence stems from the relatively few firms in the movie theater industry, and even more importantly, from the differentiated nature of the industry's products. That is, one theater's product is not the same as another's. In this environment interesting results occur such as the success of one theater featuring foreign films, but the absence of similar theaters. Collusion is another major theme, with the chapter discussing the forces encouraging or disrupting the creation and preservation of collusive agreements.

Important Concepts

Monopoly
Profit Maximization
Welfare Maximization
Average Cost Pricing
Price Discrimination
Natural Monopoly
Tax Burden
Redistribution of Income
Marginal Revenue
Marginal Cost
Average Cost
Monopoly Profit
Construction Subsidy
Household Tax
Property Tax
Model
Relevant Range
Construction Expenses
Operating Expenses

8

Eibenzile to Gossweinstein

The Economics
of a Toll Road

In the mythical kingdom of Beinnswich, situated among steep snowy crags, Prince Superclaus reigns. The half-million inhabitants are scattered among small villages and a few towns, and most earn their living by farming. There is an isolated village, Eibenzile, located in the northeastern corner of the kingdom, noteworthy mainly for its cathedral whose interior is adorned with white marble and gold. There is also a town, Gossweinstein, which is a regional marketing center for wool, charcoal, metal products, handicrafts, clothing, and many other products. Eibenzile sends to this market textiles, wine, wood, jewelry, and apples in years of abundant harvest.

For many years there have been two roads between Gossweinstein and Eibenzile. One is the Magic Carpet which is a twenty-four-mile toll road. In recent months it has been extensively improved. As a result, the roadway is now in excellent condition with the partial exception of a serviceable but rickety bridge near the midpoint of the route. The other road is the Grumbling One, so named because of its noisy and frequent rock slides. It is a toll-free, unmaintained, tortuous route of fifty-seven miles. Since the Magic Carpet and the Grumbling One are the only roads leading from Eibenzile, a traveler from that village must first go through Gossweinstein to reach other parts of Beinnswich.

The citizens of Eibenzile and Gossweinstein are considering the following two alternative ways of operating the Magic Carpet.

- Grundleschlotchen, whose ancestors are rumored to have been trolls, could own and operate the Magic Carpet for his own profit. Under this arrangement he could retain all tolls paid by Carpet users, but would have to pay all costs of Carpet operation, including those for major repairs and improvements.

Grundleschlotchen would not be empowered to impose taxes since under this approach the Magic Carpet would be operated as a private business.

- The Magic Carpet could be operated in the public trust by Fairenweather, a wealthy altruist whose prime objective would be to maximize the welfare of Eibenzile and Gossweinstein residents. Under this arrangement Fairenweather would be granted taxing powers; he would not receive a salary. Should he think it desirable, he could sustain a loss on the operation of the Carpet, but in this event he must impose taxes to cover the loss. Similarly, if he earns a profit on Carpet operation, he must distribute this profit through tax rebates to the people of the two communities.

  Fairenweather's secondary objective in operating the Carpet would be to minimize the redistribution of income among Eibenzile and Gossweinstein citizens through the Carpet's tolls, taxes, and/or tax rebates. That is, he would manage the Carpet in such a way as to minimize the flow of income from one community group to another. To achieve this objective he must strive to have those individuals who benefit from the Carpet pay for its costs, either through tolls or taxes.

A sizable debt had to be incurred to pay for the Carpet's recent improvement expenses. This debt must be assumed by the operator of the road, whether that be Fairenweather or Grundleschlotchen. The capacity of the Carpet is large relative to the demand for its use. Crowding is never so severe that travel time is increased appreciably. Neither Fairenweather nor Grundleschlotchen has perfect knowledge of future events. Both have estimated the demand for the Carpet's use and the costs of operating it. Their conclusions were similar on both counts. Since both Grundleschlotchen and Fairenweather expect conditions to remain stable for many years, the time horizons of the alternative operators are similar and long.

Grundleschlotchen and Fairenweather will maintain the Magic Carpet equally well. Both estimate that unless the toll is very low, demand for the Carpet's use will be dominated by adults traveling either on horseback or in carts pulled by horses or oxen. Since there is public sentiment for keeping the toll structure simple, both Grundleschlotchen and Fairenweather have agreed to charge a single one-way toll to adults traveling either on an animal or in a conveyance drawn by animal(s). No other tolls will be charged. Pedestrians, children, and animals per se will thus be free to use the Carpet without charge. The toll for Carpet use will be the same throughout the year; it will not vary with changes in traffic or other conditions.

1. Regardless of who operates the Magic Carpet, is it a monopoly? If so, is it a natural monopoly? The latter is defined as the situation in which one firm can produce sufficient output to satisfy the entire demand for the product and still be experiencing declining average costs.

2. Depict in Figure 8–1 the Magic Carpet's demand and cost schedules in the long run. Specifically, draw the demand, marginal

Figure 8-1

Alternative Operation of the Magic Carpet

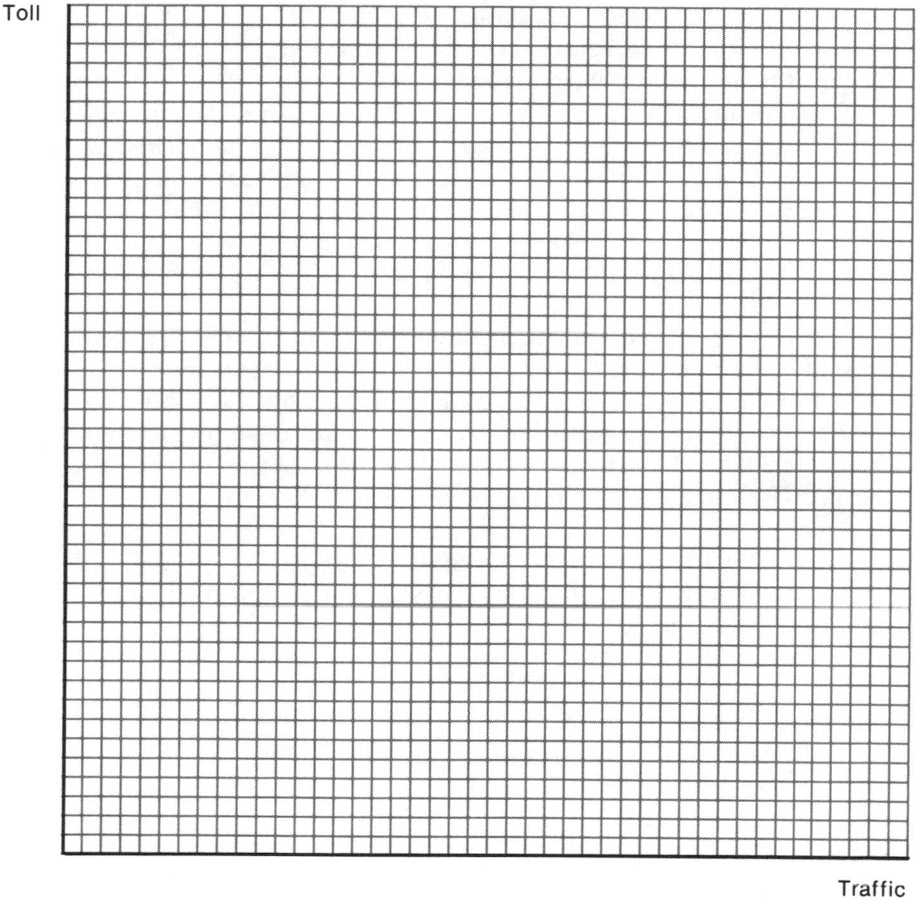

Toll

Traffic

107

revenue, marginal cost, and average cost curves. While detailed market and cost estimates have not been supplied, it is nonetheless possible to deduce the general shape of these curves from the information that has been given.

Indicate on the figure the toll that Grundleschlotchen will charge and the amount of traffic at that toll. Will he earn a profit? If so, how large will it be? Indicate on the same figure the toll that Fairenweather will charge and the amount of traffic at that toll. Will it be necessary for him to levy a tax? If so, how large must the tax be?

3. Two types of taxes are now used throughout the kingdom of Beinnswich. One is a household tax under which a specified number of beinns (the currency unit of Beinnswich) are levied annually on each adult household member under the age of seventy. The other is a property tax under which a specified percentage of the wealth of each household or business is taxed each year, with wealth defined as the value of money and property owned by the entity.

Both the household and property taxes vary across different locales of Beinnswich, but they are invariant to the personal characteristics of those being taxed within a specific locale. For example, the household tax is higher in Gossweinstein than in Eibenzile, but it is the same for all Gossweinstein households as it is the same (albeit lower than in Gossweinstein) for all Eibenzile households. The same is true for the property tax.

If it is necessary for Fairenweather to levy taxes to subsidize his operation of the Magic Carpet, which combination of these two taxes will he use for this purpose, bearing in mind that his secondary objective is to avoid a redistribution of income through his actions? Fairenweather has ruled out the possibility of establishing a new type of tax since the costs of doing so would be prohibitive.

4. To reduce barriers to commerce, Prince Superclaus proclaims a new policy under which he will pay one-half the cost of road and bridge construction in his kingdom. The Prince's new program will encourage either Grundleschlotchen or Fairenweather to replace the rickety but serviceable bridge, but what effect will it have upon the durability and size of the new bridge? Will Fairenweather's and Grundleschlotchen's responses be significantly different?

5. Both Grundleschlotchen and Fairenweather have agreed to charge the single toll described earlier for Magic Carpet travel. Suppose, however, that they revise their thinking in this area. In particular, suppose that each is free to charge different tolls to different types of users and different tolls to the same types of users at different times. In this setting consider the following three cases.

a. Wood is plentiful in Beinnswich, but apples are not. As a consequence, the value of a given weight of apples is much higher than the value of the same weight of wood. Will Fairenweather charge a higher toll to carts loaded with apples than to similar carts carrying wood? Will Grundleschlotchen follow this practice?

b. The Magic Carpet is frequently used by people traveling on horseback and by people driving carts loaded with different products. Will Grundleschlotchen charge the latter more than the former? Will Fairenweather?

c. At times people on horseback cross the Carpet on urgent personal or commercial business; at other times horseback riders traverse the Carpet for much less pressing reasons. Will Fairenweather charge the former more than the latter? Will Grundleschlotchen?

6. A third individual, Janus the Bald known for his prudence and evenhandedness, emerges and challenges both Fairenweather's and Grundleschlotchen's approaches. He argues that under Grundleschlotchen the Carpet toll will be too high and that under Fairenweather the Carpet will operate at a deficit which must be covered by taxes. Janus contends that the best alternative is to set the Carpet toll as low as possible subject to the constraint that the Carpet must not incur a deficit.

Returning to the situation where only a single toll is charged for Carpet travel, draw in Figure 8–2 (as was done earlier in Figure 8–1) the Carpet's demand, marginal revenue, marginal cost, and average cost curves in the long run. Then indicate in the figure the toll Janus will charge and the amount of traffic at that toll. Also indicate whether a profit or a loss will result from his operation.

Figure 8-2

The Magic Carpet Under Janus

Toll

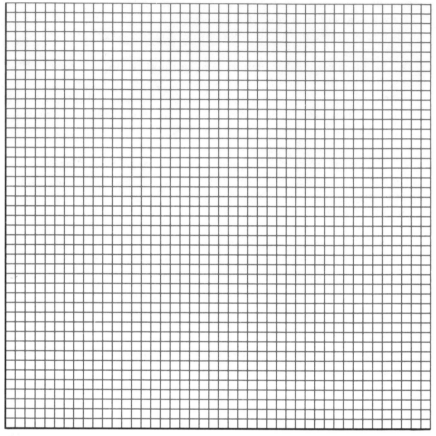

Traffic

DISCUSSION

1. Monopoly is defined as the situation in which there is only one seller or producer. It could be argued in this instance that the Magic Carpet is not a monopoly because of the presence of the Grumbling One. However, the latter is not an effective substitute for the former since it is both much longer and much more difficult to traverse. The Magic Carpet is therefore a monopoly. The definition of monopoly makes no mention about who operates the single firm in the industry. Accordingly, the toll road is a monopoly whether Grundleschlotchen or Fairenweather operates it.

The capacity of the Magic Carpet is stated to be large relative to the demand for its use. In other words, the Carpet can meet the entire market demand for road transportation services between Gossweinstein and Eibenzile. The road thus satisfies one part of the natural monopoly definition. Does it satisfy the other part? That is, does the Magic Carpet have declining average costs in the relevant range (the range of traffic volume on the Carpet which is within the realm of reasonable possibility)?

Like telephone networks, toll roads are characterized by construction expenses which are high compared to their operating costs. That is, both roads and telephone networks have high capital costs which are invariant to output. Similarly, weather damage to the Carpet does not vary with traffic. Further, some of the Carpet's operating costs which do vary with traffic do not increase proportionately with the amount of travel. This is certainly true for the expenses of collecting the tolls. It is less true for maintenance expenses, but even here there are economies of volume.

The net result of these factors is severalfold. First, at low traffic volumes the Carpet's long-run average cost will be much higher than its long-run marginal cost. Second, long-run marginal cost will be declining throughout the relevant range. Third, since long-run marginal cost is both declining and lower than average cost at low traffic volumes, long-run average cost must also be decreasing throughout the relevant range. The Magic Carpet thus meets the other part of the natural monopoly definition. It is therefore a natural monopoly.

In intuitive terms, natural monopoly refers to those situations where it is "natural" for a monopoly to develop as opposed to situations where a monopoly arises because of some type of organizational arrangement, e.g., ownership of a patent or granting of a franchise. To illustrate this point, assume that the demand for road transportation between Eibenzile and Gossweinstein doubles. Since the Carpet's capacity is large relative to the current demand, the Carpet could meet the increase in demand relatively easily. The only costs incurred by the Carpet in doubling its traffic would be an increase in maintenance costs and a smaller increment in administrative costs. In contrast, a rival road would not only experience these costs, but also large construction costs. It is therefore not economically feasible to construct a new road. This being the case, the Carpet need not resort to organizational arrangements in order to maintain its monopoly position.

2. The cost structure of the Magic Carpet was discussed in the response to the previous question. As described there and as shown in Figure 8–3, long-run marginal cost is lower than long-run average cost throughout the relevant range. The former decreases throughout that range although its rate of decline becomes very slow as traffic increases.

111

Average cost also falls throughout the relevant range with its rate of decrease being more precipitous. As traffic increases, average cost approaches marginal cost but will never equal the latter because of the Magic Carpet's substantial capital costs.

The long-run demand for Carpet use will be intermediate in elasticity throughout the relevant range. Some individuals will be willing to pay a high price to use the road, e.g., an Eibenzile craftsman wishing to transport his products to market. The demand by others for Carpet use will be much more discretionary, e.g., an Eibenzile family desiring to go to Gossweinstein to shop for clothing, handicrafts, and other items. Reflecting these considerations, the demand for Carpet use is drawn in

Figure 8-3

Alternative Operation of the Magic Carpet

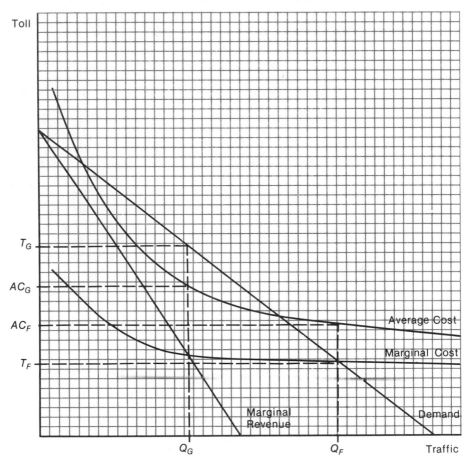

Figure 8–3 as a straight line of intermediate slope. It is acceptable and probably more accurate to depict demand as a curve, but the straight-line form is used here to illustrate the relationship between a straight-line demand curve and marginal revenue.

As discussed in earlier chapters, marginal revenue is the change in total revenue resulting from the sale of an additional unit of the product. In a perfectly competitive industry each firm is so small relative to the market that its actions do not affect market price. Marginal revenue to such a firm is therefore constant and equal to price. However, the Magic Carpet is a monopoly which faces a downward-sloping demand curve. In this situation marginal revenue does not equal price.

To determine why, consider the results when the Carpet slightly lowers its price in order to attract an additional trip. Like a firm in a perfectly competitive industry, the Carpet receives the full amount of the new price for the additional unit. However, since the Carpet charges all users the same price, it receives from its previous users not the old price, but rather the new lower price. The Carpet therefore loses the difference between the new and old prices multiplied by the number of trips at the old price.

Marginal revenue for a monopolist like the Magic Carpet thus equals the new price minus the loss on the previous trips. If the demand curve is a straight line as in this situation, the marginal revenue curve of the monopolist is also a straight line. Its negative slope is twice that of the demand curve, and it intersects the price axis at the same point as the demand curve. A marginal revenue curve with these characteristics is shown in Figure 8–3.

Since Grundleschlotchen is a profit maximizer, he will operate at the point where marginal revenue equals marginal costs. This occurs when traffic equals Q_G in Figure 8–3. To achieve this traffic level Grundleschlotchen will charge a toll equal to T_G; his average cost will be AC_G. Grundleschlotchen will earn a profit on each trip equal to the difference between the toll and average cost. His total profit will therefore equal the traffic level Q_G multiplied by the difference between the toll T_G and average cost AC_G. This profit is often termed monopoly profit since it arises from the monopoly power of the firm (the Magic Carpet in this instance).

Fairenweather's objective is to maximize the welfare of Eibenzile/Gossweinstein citizens. He should therefore operate the Carpet at a traffic level where the opportunity cost to society of an additional trip equals the marginal value placed by society on that trip. The Carpet's marginal cost curve indicates the opportunity cost to society of each additional trip. By depicting the prices which people are willing to pay for additional trips, the Carpet's demand curve indicates the marginal value placed by

113

society on additional trips. Fairenweather will therefore operate where the marginal cost curve intersects the demand curve. At that juncture the marginal cost of a trip equals its marginal value.

In Figure 8–3 the Carpet's demand and marginal cost curves intersect at traffic level Q_F. To attain this level, Fairenweather will charge a toll equal to T_F. He will sustain a loss on each trip equal to average cost AC_F minus the toll T_F. He thus must levy taxes to cover the operating deficit. They must equal the traffic level Q_F multiplied by the difference between AC_F and T_F.

The welfare maximizer Fairenweather thus operates at a larger scale than does the profit maximizer Grundleschlotchen. That is, substantially more traffic will use the Magic Carpet under Fairenweather than under Grundleschlotchen. The latter will charge a much higher price than will the former. Further, Grundleschlotchen will earn a profit while Fairenweather will sustain a loss.

These results occur because the welfare maximizer sets marginal cost equal to price, while the profit maximizer equates marginal cost and marginal revenue. While the differences between the two will vary depending upon the shapes of the demand and cost curves, the welfare maximizer will never charge a higher price or operate at a smaller volume than will the profit maximizer. Moreover, only when the demand curve facing a monopoly is perfectly elastic—a most unlikely event since the definition of monopoly excludes close substitutes—will a welfare maximizer and a profit maximizer operate a monopoly in the same way. Therefore, for practical purposes the specific results derived here can be generalized to monopolies as a whole. That is, operating a monopoly to maximize welfare will result in a lower price and a higher output than will operating the same monopoly to maximize profits.

These conclusions and others derived in this chapter are important because profit maximization and welfare maximization are major models for monopoly operation. It is true that in the modern world there are few pure examples of either. However, most contemporary monopolies combine elements of each. For example, a profit-maximizing steamship firm may be granted an exclusive license to operate a ferry route subject to the condition that it be regulated by a government authority, whose at least ostensible objective is to maximize public welfare. At a minimum a thorough grounding in the profit maximization and welfare maximization models provides a solid basis for analyzing most monopoly situations in the present world.

3. Since Fairenweather wishes to minimize the redistribution of income among Eibenzile/Gossweinstein citizens, he would prefer to levy a tax on each individual which would be proportional to the net benefit derived from the Carpet. The net benefit of the Carpet to each individual equals the valuation placed by him or her on the Carpet's services minus the tolls paid. As discussed earlier, the demand curve depicts the marginal value placed on each Carpet trip. Since the toll is constant at T_F, Fairenweather would prefer to tax each individual an amount proportional to his or her valuation of Carpet trips minus the constant toll, i.e., to levy a tax proportional to each person's consumer surplus. Further, in an ideal system Fairenweather should tax certain individuals like Gossweinstein merchants, who do not directly use the Carpet but who benefit significantly from its operation. However, even if Fairenweather could design a new taxation system based upon these considerations, the costs of setting up such a system would overwhelm the benefits from doing so.

Since Fairenweather is thus limited to the two existing taxes, which combination of these is most satisfactory for his purposes? The burden of the household tax falls evenly on all nonaged adults. In contrast, the burden of the wealth tax is borne by those who are wealthier. Who benefits more by the operation of the Carpet? That is, do the benefits of Carpet operation fall evenly across the adult population or do the wealthy benefit more than the poor?

Merchants, artisans, large farmers, and others use the Carpet for commerce. They place a higher valuation on the Carpet's services than do small farmers who travel only occasionally. Since the former are wealthier than the latter, this consideration favors the use of the property tax. However, there is another important consideration. Gossweinstein is connected by other roads to other points in Beinnswich, while the Magic Carpet is essentially the only road out of Eibenzile. The Carpet is thus more valuable to Eibenzile citizens than to Gossweinstein residents. Moreover, from this perspective the Carpet has value even to the relatively poor of Eibenzile, especially since there is no charge for Carpet travel strictly by foot.

Combining these considerations, the characteristics of Fairenweather's optimal tax package become clear. First, he should not raise the household tax in Gossweinstein. Second, the property tax should be the primary vehicle used by Fairenweather. Third, the increment in the property tax rate should be higher in Eibenzile than in Gossweinstein since, on average, Eibenzile property owners benefit more from the Carpet than do Gossweinstein property owners. Fourth, Fairenweather should raise the Eibenzile household tax to a small extent since all Eibenzile residents benefit from the Carpet to a significant degree.

The necessity for Fairenweather to set up a sound system of taxation illustrates one of the integral and more difficult aspects of welfare maximization. In comparing this model with profit maximization, it is important to go beyond an examination of the different ways that the two models will operate the industry. That is, it is not sufficient to simply state that the welfare maximizer must raise taxes equal to a certain amount without discussing the types of taxes that will be employed for this purpose.

4. Construction costs are subsidized under the Prince's policy but maintenance costs are not. Assuming that the Prince's subsidy will induce Grundleschlotchen or Fairenweather to replace the bridge, either will build a more durable bridge which will have lower maintenance costs in the future. Similarly, but to a lesser extent, the Prince's policy will encourage a shift toward larger bridges since the marginal cost of constructing a large bridge as opposed to a medium-sized bridge has now been halved.

Since Fairenweather and Grundleschlotchen envision similar demand and cost schedules for the Magic Carpet, their responses to the Prince's policy will be similar. The most likely exception to this point would arise if the construction of a large bridge would primarily affect the demand and / or cost schedules at traffic levels distinctly higher than those used by Grundleschlotchen. In this instance Fairenweather might build a substantially larger bridge than would Grundleschlotchen.

This question gains added significance because a frequent policy of the federal government in this country is to subsidize construction costs but not maintenance or other operating expenses. As is evident from this discussion, this policy encourages the target industry to overinvest in buildings and other facilities. That is, larger and / or more durable facilities are constructed than would be indicated by opportunity cost considerations. The same point applies to charitable giving. For this reason private schools often find themselves in the position of having beautiful facilities, but barely adequate operating funds.

5a. Charging different prices to different types of users or to the same types of users at different times is termed price discrimination. The rationale behind the term is that the firm is attempting to discriminate among its customers, using price as the instrument for doing so. The welfare maximizer Fairenweather will employ price discrimination at times, but he will only do so if different users impose distinctly different marginal costs on the Carpet. As described earlier, maintenance expenses comprise the largest percentage of marginal costs. Maintenance expenses vary directly with the wear and tear on the road. Fairenweather will therefore use price discrimination if one class of users routinely damages the road more than does another class. The profit-maximizing Grundleschlotchen will follow the same practice.

In addition, Grundleschlotchen will try to discriminate among his clientele on the basis of the intensity of their demand for Carpet travel. That is, he may charge a higher toll to individuals who highly value Carpet travel than to individuals who do not. By doing so he can increase his profits. Returning to Figure 8–3, price discrimination has the effect of raising marginal revenue. That is, to attract another unit of Carpet travel Grundleschlotchen need not lower his price to all previous users of the Carpet.

Fairenweather will not price discriminate on the basis of demand intensity. His main objective is to maximize the joint welfare of Eibenzile/Gossweinstein citizens. To do so he must equate marginal cost with price. If Fairenweather charges a group of users a price higher than the marginal cost that they impose on the Carpet, he will violate his main objective, even though from the standpoint of avoiding income redistribution he might prefer to cover the Carpet's deficit partly through price discrimination, rather than entirely through taxation.

In this case equally heavy apple and wood carts damage the roadway to the same extent. There is thus no reason for Grundleschlotchen or Fairenweather to impose price discrimination because of marginal cost differences. However, a cargo of apples is distinctly more valuable than a cargo of wood. It is therefore likely that a person with a cart full of apples more highly values Carpet travel than does an individual with a cart full of wood. That is, it is probable that the former's demand for Carpet travel is greater than the latter's. This being the case, and presuming that the trade in apples and wood is sufficient to make it worth his while, Grundleschlotchen will place a higher toll on carts laden with apples than on carts loaded with wood. Fairenweather will not adopt this practice since he will not impose price discrimination to capture differences in demand.

5b. Individuals driving carts impose much higher marginal costs on the Carpet than do people on horseback. Further, on average, the former have a stronger demand for Carpet use than do the latter. The result of both factors is that Grundleschlotchen and Fairenweather will charge a higher toll to individuals driving carts than to people on horseback, but the difference between the tolls to the two groups will be greater for Grundleschlotchen.

5c. This case brings up another issue central to price discrimination. To effectively discriminate on the basis of a particular characteristic, a firm must be able to readily distinguish among its customers in terms of the characteristic. This is not possible in this situation. The distinguishing characteristic here is the motive of the traveler. Neither Grundleschlotchen nor Fairenweather (nor even more so, their employees) can easily discern a traveler's motive. Neither will therefore charge a higher price to individuals on urgent business than to individuals traveling for less pressing reasons.

6. The model proposed by Janus calls for the toll to be as low as possible so long as a deficit is not incurred. The toll must therefore equal average cost. This situation is portrayed in Figure 8–4. The toll is T_J, which also equals the average cost. At that toll traffic equals Q_J. There is

Figure 8–4

The Magic Carpet Under Average Cost Pricing

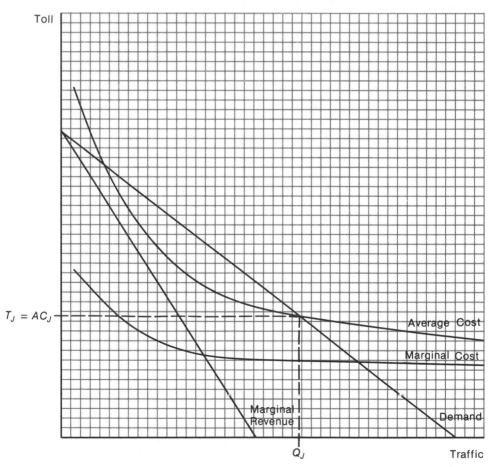

neither a profit nor a deficit since both are ruled out by the conditions of this model.

This model is termed average cost pricing. In this situation it results in a toll which is intermediate between those of profit maximization and welfare maximization. Similarly, it produces an output intermediate between those of the other models. These differences between average cost pricing and profit maximization hold for any monopoly (except in the most unlikely instance when demand is perfectly elastic). That is, average cost pricing will yield a lower price and a higher output than will profit maximization.

However, the differences observed here between average cost pricing and welfare maximization may or may not hold in other monopolies. In most natural monopolies the results will be as they are here. That is, average cost pricing will produce a higher price and a lower output than will welfare maximization. However, in some monopolies, especially those created by government action or by another organizational arrangement, marginal cost is rising and greater than average cost within part of the relevant range. In such cases average cost pricing may produce a lower price and a greater output than will welfare maximization.

Average cost pricing is commonly practiced in the United States. The most visible example is utility regulation in which rates are set equal to average costs, with a so-called fair rate of return on the firm's investment included in the calculation of costs. Compared to welfare maximization, average cost pricing is less satisfactory from the standpoint that price does not equal marginal cost. However, it has the salient advantage that average cost is much easier to measure than marginal cost. Also, as in the Magic Carpet case, welfare maximization can result in a price which does not cover average cost. If so, it will be necessary to subsidize the operation of the utility or other monopoly with tax revenues—a step which is likely to be quite unpopular.

Still another point, which is also applicable to welfare maximization, is that average cost pricing changes the incentives facing the firm. Under profit maximization there is an incentive to be more efficient, to reduce costs, and to thereby increase profits. Often one result of this process, even in the monopoly situation, is a lower price to consumers. In contrast, under average cost pricing an expense will be paid as long as it is allowable in the calculation of cost. There is thus no incentive to reduce costs. In fact, there may be an incentive to raise costs, especially expenses for items valued by the firm's management. Such items may range from executive perquisites to technological hardware.

Important Concepts

Differentiated Oligopoly
Product Differentiation
Small Number of Producers
Interdependence of Oligopolists
Independence of Perfect Competitors
Uncertainty of Oligopoly
Location Effects
Extent of Market
Economic Profit
Price Reaction
Price Discrimination
Economies of Volume
Increasing Returns to Scale
Collusion
Gains from Collusion
Price Breaking
Price Shading
Freedom of Entry
Interloper
Instability of Collusion
Cartel
Pure Oligopoly
Monopolistic Competition

9

Cinema in Skikamagua

The Dynamic World
of Differentiated Oligopoly

Skikamagua is a hypothetical but realistic city in the state of Washington. It is the focal point of the surrounding region; there is no city within one hundred miles which has a population larger than 75,000. Skikamagua grew up as a marketing center for agricultural products, and this is still an important activity. Wheat is the dominant crop grown by the area's farmers, but other products are also important, including hay, potatoes, fruits, and beef. Mining has also been a traditional activity in the area, and this remains true at present. During the last half century, but especially during the past two decades, many commercial and industrial firms have moved to Skikamagua, have established major branches there, or have flourished after being initiated there. As a result of these developments, Skikamagua is now a prosperous city with a diversified economic base.

Approximately 500,000 people live in the Skikamagua metropolitan area. Located in the area are two colleges with their attendant activities, a small art museum, a somewhat larger natural history museum, and a zoo with a modest but well-presented collection. There are numerous restaurants, bars, discotheques, and other nightclubs. The city has no major league sports teams, but there are several minor league teams. The surrounding area features a wealth of recreational opportunities, including skiing, fishing, boating, hunting, and camping. Within the metropolitan area are well-maintained parks, municipal tennis courts, racquet clubs, bowling alleys, and golf courses.

The Skikamagua metropolitan area contains 44 movie theaters, defined as separate screening areas. Six of these are drive-in theaters and 27 of the remaining 38 share a common facility with at least one other theater. These theaters exhibit a wide range of films, but only rarely

X-rated features. Fourteen firms comprise the Skikamagua cinema industry. All are independent and there is no formal connection among them. No firm operates more than 7 theaters, but the largest six firms are responsible for 32 theaters.

Skikamagua also has 6 "adult theaters" which customarily show X-rated films. The three firms which own these theaters are independent of each other. They are also not formally associated with any of the fourteen firms which operate the regular movie theaters.

A special license is not required to operate a regular movie theater in Skikamagua. Similarly, there are no unusual zoning or other restrictions impeding entry into the retail movie business. As in many cities, an informal agreement exists between government officials and adult theater owners. As long as the latter's behavior remains restrained especially in terms of advertising and choice of location, the former will not significantly constrain the operation of adult theaters.

1. Do the theaters of Skikamagua, or their fourteen owners, produce the same product? If not, how do the products differ?

2. The Deerwood Twin and the Lakeview II are theaters located within two miles of each other in eastern Skikamagua. Both exhibit largely first-run films, and both have two screening areas. The two establishments are not owned by the same firm. Jeff MacGregor and Rick Stevensen own medium-sized farms which are adjacent to each other twenty-five miles from Skikamagua. The primary product of each farmer is wheat which is sold in the Skikamagua regional market.

If the Deerwood lowers its ticket prices, will the Lakeview be concerned? If Jeff reduces his wheat prices, will Rick be concerned?

3. Based upon the responses to the previous questions, which theoretical market structure most closely characterizes the Skikamagua movie industry—perfect competition, monopoly, monopolistic competition, pure oligopoly, or differentiated oligopoly?

4. The Esquire Theater, located near one of the colleges in Skikamagua, features outstanding foreign films. Its owner, David Carpello, has consistently earned economic profits. Most of the land in the Esquire's neighborhood is presently in use, but it would be possible either to convert an existing building into a theater or to purchase a vacant lot and build a theater. However, no present or prospective theater owners have any plans to construct a theater similar to the Esquire. At times other Skikamagua theaters show high-quality foreign films, but they do not make a standard practice of doing so. Skikamagua theater owners have not established a collusive agreement which might protect the Esquire's market position.

What is the explanation for this apparently contradictory phenomenon? That is, given that the Esquire Theater consistently earns economic profits, why have new entrants similar to the Esquire not been attracted to the theater industry?

5. The Hilltop Theater is located in northeastern Skikamagua, not too far from the Deerwood Twin and Lakeview II. Faced with rising costs, the Hilltop is considering an approximate 10 percent price increase. Compare the effects of this contemplated action on the number of tickets sold by the Hilltop in two situations. First, assume that other theaters do not change their ticket prices; and second, assume that other theaters emulate the Hilltop's behavior and raise their prices by about 10 percent.

6. As in other American communities, the movie theaters in Skikamagua charge one price for adults and a much lower price for children. Why do they follow this practice?

7. Throughout the United States there has been a shift away from single-theater buildings and toward multitheater facilities. This same trend is evident in Skikamagua. What advantages do multitheater facilities have compared to single-theater buildings? What disadvantages?

8. The Festival and Continental theater chains are the largest in Skikamagua. Their owners meet for a long lunch to discuss matters of mutual interest. Although not stated in such terms, in reality the focus of their discussions is the possibility of forming a collusive agreement among Skikamagua theater owners. If this possibility comes to fruition, the owners would cooperate and the industry would be operated according to the terms of the agreement. An agreement of this type is illegal in the United States. Why then are the Festival and Continental owners devoting careful attention to the possibility of establishing such an agreement?

9. Over the course of several months the Continental and Festival theater owners continue to explore the possibility of forming a collusive agreement. Each owner talks with theater owners that he knows particularly well. Eventually an evening session is held at the home of the Festival Theater owner. Its explicit but unannounced purpose is to seriously consider the formation of a collusive agreement in the Skikamagua theater industry. The participants at the session are the six largest theater owners who together control 32 of the area's 44 theaters.

If a collusive agreement is formed, should these six owners endeavor to bring within it the four single-theater firms in Skikamagua? Should they strive to include the three firms which control the 6 adult theaters in Skikamagua?

10. After three months of extensive and at times painful negotiations, a collusive agreement is concluded which involves the ten largest theater firms in Skikamagua. The agreement specifies ticket prices in terms of five variables: location of the theater, general classification of the featured film, whether the film is a first or subsequent-run showing, the time of the showing, and the age of the ticket buyer. The colluding parties may charge prices higher than those specified in the agreement, but they may not charge prices which are lower. During the negotiation process the theater owners considered including other items in the agreement, but eventually decided not to.

a. Once the agreement is in force, is there an incentive for the colluding parties to violate the agreement and charge lower prices?

b. What impact will the agreement have on the prices of food and drinks sold at theater snack bars? On the number of theaters offering free parking for patrons at nearby facilities?

c. When might it be profitable for a colluding firm to charge higher prices than those specified in the agreement? Would the firm's fellow colluders object to this practice?

11. After the collusive agreement has been in effect for about a year, a new theater operated by a new firm opens in Skikamagua. It is the well-constructed Casteel Theater which features twin screening areas. Its owner, Bianca Balthazer, was not a party to the collusive agreement, but has since become aware of its existence.

Is it likely that Bianca will expose the colluders and complain that she is being exploited by the colluding group? Is it likely that the colluding group will attempt to induce Bianca to join the collusive agreement? If so, is she likely to accept?

DISCUSSION

1. The products of movie theaters, and thus of their fourteen owners in Skikamagua, are clearly different. They differ along several dimensions, but the two most important are the specific film being shown and the location of the theater. When firms in an industry produce products with different characteristics, the industry is said to be characterized by product differentiation. An equally accurate term would be product heterogeneity.

A major assumption of the perfectly competitive model is product homogeneity. The violation of this assumption alone means that each firm in a differentiated industry faces a downward-sloping demand curve, albeit the downward slope may be only slight. That being the case, a firm with a differentiated product cannot take price as a constant which will not be impacted by its actions. Rather, such a firm must be cognizant that the price it will receive will be influenced by the amount it sells.

In some cases product differentiation may be more apparent than real. For example, despite advertising claims to the contrary, the quality of different aspirin tablets may be quite similar. Reflecting this phenomenon, product differentiation has at times been applied to those situations where advertising and other marketing techniques are employed to exaggerate differences among basically similar products.

Product differentiation is used in a more generic sense in this book. The term simply denotes those situations where consumers see significant differences in an industry's products, whether those differences be intrinsic to the industry or largely created by advertising. The former is true in the Skikamagua movie industry. While some theaters can be located in the same place and while some can exhibit the same film, it will not be profitable for all theaters to be in the same place and to show the same film at the same time. Product differentiation is inescapable in the retail movie industry. The same applies to many industries, especially at the retail level.

2. While both operate medium-sized farms, Jeff and Rick are small producers in a large regional market. Further, both produce agricultural commodities which are considered by the market to be uniform within a few quality grades. As a result of both factors, neither farmer is able to influence the prevailing conditions in the Skikamagua market. The two farmers are therefore independent of each other. The actions of one do not influence the situation of the other. That being the case, Rick may wonder why Jeff is lowering his price, but he will not be concerned since Jeff's action will not influence the prices that Rick receives for his products.

In contrast, Skikamagua movie theaters produce related but still different products, and there are only fourteen firms in the industry. The consequence of both factors is that no theater firm is small relative to the Skikamagua cinema market. That is, even for the single-theater firms, the actions of one firm will appreciably influence the situation of at least one other firm in the industry. Further, the Deerwood and Lakeview theaters are not miles apart nor do they show drastically different films. Rather, they are close competitors in terms of both location and types of movies. The actions of one will have a substantial impact on the situation of the other. That is, the two theaters are strongly interdependent.

The Lakeview will thus be quite concerned about any significant action that the Deerwood takes. A ticket price reduction would certainly be placed in that category by the Lakeview, since it could substantially influence the demand for the Lakeview's products. The Lakeview would therefore carefully consider the Deerwood's action and would probably mount a response of some kind.

3. One condition of perfect competition holds in the Skikamagua movie industry—freedom of entry. Another is probably also satisfied: widespread knowledge of market conditions by buyers and sellers. However, the other two conditions are violated. Each firm is not small relative to the market, and the theaters do not produce a homogeneous product.

The Skikamagua cinema industry is clearly not a monopoly since there are fourteen firms, rather than one. It is also not a pure oligopoly since its products are differentiated.

Although less well defined than perfect competition, monopolistic competition is generally described as meeting three conditions. First, the products of the industry must be differentiated but still close substitutes. Second, there must be a large number of firms in the industry so that each firm presumes that its actions will not influence its counterparts. Third, the firms in the industry must face the same demand and cost curves. The last condition is highly restrictive and need not hold even in perfect competition. The model of monopolistic competition has been legitimately attacked on this point. Certainly in the Skikamagua movie industry there is no reason to suspect that the firms have identical demand and cost curves.

Even beyond this conflict with the monpolistic competition model, the number of firms in the Skikamagua movie industry is not so large that each firm would presume that its actions would have a negligible effect on its fellows. The industry is thus not characterized by monopolistic competition.

Differentiated oligopoly has two central characteristics, both of which are indicated by its name. First, there must be a small number of producers. Each firm therefore presumes correctly that its actions will have an impact on its counterparts. Second, the industry must be characterized by product differentiation. As discussed in the previous questions, both these conditions hold in the Skikamagua movie industry. That industry is therefore a differentiated oligopoly.

This characterization of the Skikamgua movie industry is accurate even though the number of firms, fourteen, is perhaps larger than the common perception of oligopoly. However, the critical factor is not the absolute number of firms, but rather whether the firms are interdependent. That is, do the actions of one firm influence the situation of others?

The interdependence of oligopolists is a striking feature. It contrasts sharply with the independence of perfect competitors. This interdependence makes the oligopolist's world both dynamic and uncertain. A firm in a perfectly competitive industry must carefully evaluate expected future market conditions, but it need not worry about the actions of specific counterparts. The monopolist constitutes the entire industry and by definition substitutes are at least somewhat distant. In either monopoly or perfect competition the central concern is the market as a whole. Change is usually gradual across the entire market for a product. In distinct contrast, the market conditions confronting an oligopolist can change quickly because of competitors' actions. At a minimum the potential for such change is always present. As a consequence, the worlds of perfect competition and monopoly are serene compared to the world of oligopoly.

4. A positive economic profit means that the firm is earning a higher rate of return than it could in alternative pursuits. That being the case, entrepreneurs will attempt to emulate the firm. The presence of economic profits thus induces entrepreneurs to enter the industry—a process which continues in the traditional case until economic profits are driven to zero.

Why does this phenomenon not occur in the Esquire's case? The factor responsible is the extent of the market. The market for outstanding foreign films is large enough to permit the Esquire to make an economic profit, but it is not sufficiently large to support two theaters specializing in such films. Other theaters can garner some of the Esquire's profits by showing foreign films. However, it will be difficult for them to seriously erode the Esquire's profits for three reasons. First, the Esquire's location is probably well suited to an emphasis on foreign films. That is, its location confers significant benefits on the Esquire. Second, by specializing the Esquire has gained a reputation and consequently consumers who like foreign films will look first to the Esquire. Third, the Esquire's specialization has also probably enabled the owner David Carpello to establish a series of fruitful contacts and contracts in the foreign film area.

127

This question illustrates the general point that even at long-run equilibrium in a differentiated oligopoly some firms may be earning economic profits. Further, they may be earning these profits even though entry into the industry is unrestricted, as is true in the Skikamagua cinema industry. In the Esquire's case the factor responsible for the theater's economic profits is the extent of the market for foreign films. However, other factors can also lead to economic profits. For example, a theater owner may have a unique talent for selecting films that will be favorably received by the public. If so, he or she will earn an economic profit even at long-run equilibrium.

5. If other theaters do not change their ticket prices, the impact of the Hilltop's contemplated price increase on the number of tickets sold by the theater will be much larger than if other theaters institute comparable price increases. This point is illustrate in Figure 9–1. P_0 is the current price charged by the Hilltop, and Q_0 is the number of tickets sold by the theater at that price. D_0 is the Hilltop's demand curve assuming that all other theaters keep their prices constant at the current rates. In contrast, D_{10} is the Hilltop's demand curve assuming that all other theaters approximately match price changes made by the Hilltop.

The difference between the demand curves is due entirely to the price reaction of the Hilltop's competitors. If they do not react at all, the Hilltop's demand curve is much more elastic than if they fully react. Accordingly, if the Hilltop raises its price by 10 percent from P_0 to P_1 and if other theaters do not increase their prices, the quantity of tickets sold by the Hilltop will decline sharply from Q_0 to Q_1. However, if other theaters also execute approximate 10 percent price increases, the impact of the Hilltop's price increase will be much more modest: The quantity of tickets sold will decrease from Q_0 to Q_2.

Figure 9–1 points up the uncertainty facing a firm in a differentiated oligopoly. If the Hilltop's competitors do not increase their prices in response to the Hilltop's move and/or because of similar cost pressures, it may not be economically feasible for the Hilltop to raise its prices even though its costs are rising. If, however, the Hilltop's rivals also envision a price increase, it may be highly advantageous for the Hilltop to institute its price change. It is thus advisable for the Hilltop to ascertain its rivals' thinking in this area, especially the plans of its close competitors, perhaps the Deerwood Twin and Lakeview II.

This point holds generally in an oligopoly. Considerable effort is therefore devoted to making and maintaining contacts in the industry and to obtaining pertinent information through either direct exchange or more circuitous routes.

Figure 9-1

Impact of Price Reaction on Hilltop's Demand

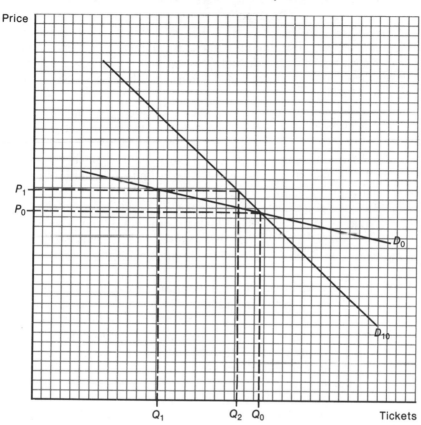

6. This pricing practice is a form of price discrimination. Although the adult/child distinction is the most common type of price discrimination in the retail movie industry, theaters also employ other types, such as charging different prices for different films and charging an intermediate price to students and/or the elderly.

Price discrimination may be employed in some situations because the marginal costs of providing services to two types of customers are substantially different. However, this is not the case here. The marginal cost to a theater of admitting an adult is highly similar to that of admitting a child. If anything, children may impose greater costs on theaters than do adults.

However, as discussed in the previous chapter, price discrimination can be profitable if two types of customers have distinctly different demands for the product and if one type can be easily distinguished from the other. Both conditions hold for the adult/child price discrimination practiced by theaters. With the exception of children near the age boundary, a child can be readily distinguished from an adult. Adults have a greater demand for movies than do children. More important, charging a lower price for children enables theaters to discriminate between strictly adult clientele and families. For several reasons, including the larger size of the group, families usually have a more elastic demand than do adults.

There is another condition for successful price discrimination that was not mentioned in the previous chapter. It is that consumers must not be able to easily transfer the product among themselves. If they can do so, the discriminatory price structure will collapse since consumers offered the product at the lower price will resell it to consumers restricted to the higher price.

Transfer of the product among consumers is clearly not feasible for the toll road users in Chapter 8. Similarly, it is not an important factor in the retail movie industry since such transfer can be easily discouraged by selling tickets which differ in color and other characteristics.

7. It is less costly to construct a multitheater facility than the same number of theaters in separate buildings. Even more important, a multitheater facility enables certain inputs to be used more fully and thus more efficiently. The separate screening areas can be serviced by the same parking lots, refreshment stands, rest rooms, and ushers/ticket sellers. Although present to a degree even if movie starting times are identical, the economies in the joint use of these resources can be markedly enhanced by coordinating starting times.

The greater volume passing through a multitheater facility produces another advantage. It becomes possible to add decorative attractions which would not be economically feasible in a single-theater building. For example, installing a fountain in the lobby of a three-theater facility might attract consumers and thus be a profitable move. Such a step might well be too costly in terms of the traffic passing through a single-theater facility.

The cost savings produced by multitheater facilities are an example of economies of volume. The economies arise because all inputs need not be increased proportionately in a multitheater facility. For example, rest room capacity does not have to be twice as large in a twin theater as in a single theater. Strictly speaking, the multitheater facility is thus not an example of increasing returns to scale, which entail disproportionately more output being produced by an equiproportional increase in all inputs.

130

The chief disadvantage of multitheater facilities is that the theaters are located in the same place. Owners of such facilities must therefore carefully consider location effects in selecting suitable sites. It is important that such facilities be situated at points where consumer demand is high. Demand may be high simply because an area is densely populated. More frequently, it is high because of easy transportation access. Large shopping centers are often excellent sites for multitheater facilities since they combine ample parking with proximity to major transportation routes.

The trend toward multitheater facilities was accelerated by the development of the interstate highway system and city freeways feeding into that system. They made it possible for residents of metropolitan areas to comfortably travel considerable distances to see a movie. It is therefore likely that the shift toward multitheater facilities will be slowed or perhaps reversed in part by the decreasing availability of gasoline and the concomitant increase in gasoline prices.

8. By colluding the Skikamagua theater owners can increase the total profits of their industry. They can do so because if they cooperate they can operate the industry more like a monopoly. Since substantial profit can be made in this way, oligopolists like these two theater owners are at times willing to collude, even though they run the risk of prosecution under the antitrust laws should their activities come to light.

In contrast to the United States, collusive agreements are legal in many European countries. If it is legal, the cooperative management of an industry by oligopolists is usually termed a cartel.

9. The disadvantage of not including the four small firms in the agreement is that it will reduce the total gains that can be attained through collusion. However, this reduction may be modest since the four firms control only about 10 percent of Skikamagua's theaters.

On the other side of the ledger, leaving these firms outside the agreement has two advantages which may be substantial. First, the agreement is illegal. Therefore, the fewer parties involved, the better from the standpoint of keeping the agreement secret. Second, for collusion to succeed not only must the total profits of the industry be increased, but also the individual profits of each firm involved. If its profits are not increased by the collusive arrangement, a firm will not join the collusive group. Reducing the number of theater owners involved from 14 to 10 will thus diminish the negotiation required to conclude the collusive agreement.

On balance, it is likely to be inadvisable for the larger theater owners to endeavor to include the single-theater firms. However, there are

131

exceptions to this point. For example, the owner of a single-theater firm could be quite influential in the industry for personal/professional reasons. Or, a single-theater firm could have an excellent location and thus be considered a strong competitor by one or more of the large firms.

Regular movies and adult films are not close substitutes. There is thus little to be lost by leaving the three adult theater firms outside the collusive agreement. Since increasing the number of people involved has the disadvantages described above, the six theater owners should make no effort to include the adult theater firms in the collusive agreement.

10a. In the collusive situation a firm can substantially increase its profits by lowering its prices, presuming that its fellow colluders do not lower theirs. There is thus an incentive for any colluding theater to break the terms of the agreement. However, there are disincentives as well. A colluding theater cannot be certain that its fellows will remain impassive and leave their prices unchanged. Instead, they may retaliate by reducing their prices. Further, if the rest of the colluding group maintains a strong front, they can selectively reduce their prices in ways that will make the position of the price breaker quite uncomfortable.

Violation of the collusive agreement through price breaking is therefore somewhat unlikely. This likelihood is further reduced in the Skikamagua cinema industry because ticket prices are posted. It is thus easy for the colluders to detect price violations by their fellows.

10b. The agreement places no restrictions on snack bar prices or fringes offered by theaters, such as free parking. Prior to the agreement theaters competed in these areas, but they also competed in terms of the usually more important variable, ticket price. Since the agreement limits competition in the latter area, competition will increase in the former areas after the agreement. Each theater will strive to increase its demand by lowering its snack bar prices and by offering free parking and other fringes. The agreement will thus reduce snack bar prices and increase the number of theaters offering free parking.

Both the decreases in snack bar prices and the increases in fringes are forms of price shading. They reduce the total price of the movie entertainment package, even though they do not alter the price of the major component. Price shading is common in a collusive situation. Compared to an overt price reduction, it accomplishes at least some of the same objectives; and it has the distinct advantage of either being permissible under the collusive agreement, as in this case, or of being less obvious to the firm's fellow colluders.

10c. In general, each theater would prefer to charge a lower price than that specified in the agreement, presuming again that its fellow colluders abide by the agreement. However, if the demand for a specific movie is overwhelmingly high as was the case for *Star Wars* in the late 1970s, the theater involved may be able to increase its profits by charging prices higher than the minimums established in the agreement. If the theater does so, its fellow colluders will not object since the higher price for the popular film will shift at least a few moviegoers to other theaters.

11. The term interloper is often bestowed on a firm entering a collusive industry. The interloper in this situation, the Casteel Theater, is in the fortunate position of being able to charge whatever prices it thinks best, while all but its single-theater competitors are limited to the prices specified in the agreement. The Casteel is like an original colluder who can institute an overt price reduction without provoking a similar response by its fellow colluders. The collusive agreement thus increases the profits of the Casteel Theater. Bianca is therefore unlikely to expose the colluders.

The colluding owners may think it is in their interests to extend the agreement to the Casteel. However, they may find it difficult to do so. As discussed above, the collusion in the theater industry increases the Casteel's profits. Bianca will not join the colluding group unless she can earn more by doing so than by staying outside. Since the Casteel is only a single twin theater, the colluding owners may conclude that it is not worth their while to negotiate an agreement with Bianca.

Either way the entry of the Casteel makes the colluding group worse off. If the new theater operates outside the agreement, the profits of the colluders will fall because the demand for their products will decline. If the Casteel is brought into the agreement, a portion of the colluders' profits must be explicitly or implicitly transferred to the Casteel in order to induce Bianca to join the colluding group.

The appearance of the interloper emphasizes the importance of entry to the success of collusion over time. If the colluding group cannot at least partially restrict entry into the industry, it will be hard pressed to maintain its monopoly profits. This principle clearly holds in a pure oligopoly since there are no practical differences in the products produced. It is also applicable to a differentiated oligopoly although not quite to the same extent. The product differences alone may partially protect some of the colluders from the entry of new firms.

The factors discussed in the last several answers all contribute to the instability of collusion. Price shading may become rampant forcing the colluders to abandon their agreement. The entry of new firms may steadily erode the colluders' profits. Although less common, overt price breaking may lead to the dissolution of the colluding group. Further, the illegality of collusion compounds these problems. For example, even if the antitrust laws are not stringently enforced, their presence makes it inadvisable for the colluders to commit to writing a binding contract which would eliminate certain types of price shading.

However, the instability of collusion does not mean that it is not profitable. A collusive agreement need not be maintained for years in order for the colluders to make substantial profits. Illustrating this point, the Festival and Continental theater owners could well have felt at the time of their initial conversation that their efforts would be more than justified if the collusive agreement remained in effect for a single year, if during that time price shading was moderate but not extensive, and if during that year only one or two new theaters were established in Skikamagua. Since these three conditions are well within the realm of possibility, it is clear why collusion remains attractive to oligopolists despite its potential difficulties.

IV

ALLOCATION OF PRODUCTIVE RESOURCES

Earlier chapters concentrated on the market for final products, whether they be houses, cookies, or toll road usage. This emphasis is well placed since the demand for productive resources is derived from the demand for final products. However, the workings of input markets—the subject of this section—has a crucial influence on both the supply of final products and the distribution of income among productive resources.

The dominant productive resource in most industries in labor. This characteristic holds in the Indianapolis hospital industry, the subject of Chapter 10. Hospitals are complex institutions which use a wide variety of inputs. As such, they illustrate many facets of input markets. For example, there are the radiologists who appear to be earning more, but working less. Further, there is the peculiar shortage of nurses that is a chronic hospital complaint. That is, hospitals cannot hire as many nurses as they would like at the current wage, but they are not willing to raise the wage to attract more nurses. And then there is unionization—a development less common in the hospital industry than in certain others, but important nonetheless. Will establishment of a union shop raise the wage of nurses without decreasing the number employed? Will it accomplish the same results for laundry workers?

Not all but most endeavors involve different events at different times. It is therefore essential to take into account the influence of time. Chapter 11 examines this issue, analyzing the impact of time on the production of Douglas fir. It emphasizes that like all valuable inputs, time has a price. The method for calculating the present value of a revenue or cost expected in a future time period is described in this chapter. That is, the chapter shows how to answer the question: How much is a $100 payment five years from now worth today? In addition, the chapter analyzes the impact of other important factors, including risk of fire loss, changes in timber quality, and multiple uses of the forest.

Chapter 12 is addressed to perhaps the toughest social issue: Who gets what? That is, the chapter is directed toward the distribution of income among productive resources. The consequences of a major event are not the same or even similar for the individuals comprising a population. Instead, some gain while others lose. The energy crisis is used to illustrate this fundamental premise. As discussed in Chapter 12, its fallout is wide-ranging, affecting people as disparate as California film producers, West Virginia railroad owners, Utah scientists, and Louisiana roustabouts.

Important Concepts

Competitive Input Market
Oligopsony
Derived Demand
Marginal Revenue Product
Insurance Principle
Backward-bending Supply Curve
Income Effect
Substitution Effect
Marginal Value of Leisure
Marginal Value of Work Satisfaction
Elasticity of Input Demand
Input Demand Elasticity Over Time
Relative Importance to Firm
Marginal Cost of Labor
Paradox of Oligopsonist
Heterogeneity of Labor Markets
Unionization
Open Shop
Union Shop
Excess Supply
Discrimination
Wage Shading
Monopsony
Value Marginal Product

10

Nurses and Laundry Workers

A Diversity
of Input Markets

Located near the center of Indiana, Indianapolis is the capital of the state—a role for which it was designed since its inception. The metropolitan area contains more than one million people, with more than half of these residing in Indianapolis itself. In health care as in most other fields, Indianapolis is the focal point of the state's activities. This is especially true for specialized hospital and medical care where Indianapolis serves as the referral center for the state.

There are seven large general hospitals in the metropolitan area, all of which are located in or near Indianapolis itself. Each of these hospitals has more than 400 beds; each offers a full range of diagnostic and therapeutic services; and each has at least 900 employees. Two smaller general hospitals are situated in Indianapolis, while seven such hospitals are located in the outlying sections of the metropolitan area.

Approximately 2,000 physicians practice in the Indianapolis area. Some are based exclusively in hospitals, while others work in large group practices. However, the majority practice either alone or in small groups of two or three physicians. Like other metropolitan areas, Indianapolis also has many dentists, numerous pharmacies, several psychiatric facilities, and a sizable number of nursing homes.

In Indianapolis as elsewhere, hospitals optimize across an array of objectives, including the types of services offered and the quality of care. However, they also face financial pressures—a factor accentuated in Indiana by the active presence of a regulatory program which reviews and sets hospital rates. As a consequence, while all Indianapolis hospitals are nonprofit institutions, they are sufficiently concerned about not exceeding their projected budgets that their actions frequently resemble those of profit maximizers. At the least Indianapolis hospitals have a clear incentive to restrain costs. Similarly, Indianapolis physicians optimize across a range of objectives, but profit or income is sufficiently central in their plans that they act in many ways like profit maximizers.

As in other chapters using actual examples, the questions in this chapter are hypothetical but nonetheless solidly grounded in reality.

1. In 1966 the Medicare Act previously passed by Congress was implemented nationwide. This act created a public insurance program under which the federal government paid most hospital and other health care expenses for the elderly (defined as those over sixty-four years of age). Although many of the elderly had some type of private hospital insurance before 1966, the advent of the Medicare program not only shifted the locus of hospital insurance for the elderly from the private to the public sector, but also substantially expanded the extent of such coverage.

Aside from nursing care itself, most diagnostic and therapeutic services provided by hospitals are grouped under the term ancillary services. Except in unusual hospitals, the two largest ancillary service departments are laboratory and radiology. The former is responsible for the myriad of mostly diagnostic tests which range from urinalyses to blood iron determinations. The latter provides both diagnostic and therapeutic X-ray services. Central to the operations of both departments is the technician, who personally performs many procedures and supervises the work of assistants less trained than he or she.

What was the impact of the Medicare program on the demand by Indianapolis hospitals for X-ray and laboratory technicians?

2. The last fifteen years have witnessed increasing governmental and private insurance coverage of hospital care, with the Medicare program being the most prominent example. This time span has also seen the progressive development of radiation technologies, especially for the treatment of cancer, but also for diagnostic purposes. Further, there has been an increasing emphasis on monitoring and improving the quality of hospital care. The combined result of these developments has been a sharp increase in hospital demand for radiologists—physicians with specialized training in radiology, a branch of medicine centering on the diagnostic and therapeutic use of X-ray procedures. To secure board certification in radiology, a college graduate must complete four years of medical school and another four years of specialized postgraduate training.

As elsewhere in the country, payments by Indianapolis hospitals to radiologists have increased dramatically. Yet Indianapolis hospitals still have trouble securing sufficient radiologist services. Further, the hospitals note that an increase in their payments to radiologists does not generate an increase in radiologist availability. The hospitals feel that the problem is severe enough to warrant the conduct of a radiologist survey.

Upon its completion several months later, this survey concludes that as compared to five years ago, and taking into account the effects of inflation, radiologists are working a shorter work week and their effective hourly wage is much higher. Do the survey findings provide a logical explanation for the radiologist shortage experienced by Indianapolis hospitals?

3. Natural gas prices have increased sharply in Indianapolis as they have throughout the country, especially in the Midwest and East. As yet no constraints have been placed on the availability of natural gas to institutional customers in Indianapolis. Hospitals in the area have no choice but to accept these price increases since they are too small to bargain with the utility companies. However, they can change the quantities of natural gas that they use for heating and other purposes. Assume for simplicity that the major increase in natural gas prices occurs at the present time and that it was largely unexpected. Compare the impact of this price increase on the quantity of natural gas used by an Indianapolis hospital two months from now with its effect on the quantity used two years from now.

4. The rise in petroleum prices not only increases the price of gasoline, but also the price of petrochemicals. The latter are used in the production of disposable syringes, tubing, and other items used extensively by Indianapolis hospitals. The increase in petroleum prices thus leads to a rise in the prices of these disposable items. Physician offices also use these disposable items but to a much lesser extent than do hospitals. Compare the effect of this price increase on the quantity of disposable items used by hospitals with its impact on the quantity used by physician offices.

5. While the educational backgrounds of nurses vary considerably, all have received specialized training designed to make them skilled health care professionals. As elsewhere, while nursing homes, physician offices, and other organizations use nurses, hospitals are the dominant employers of nurses in the Indianapolis area. Hospitals also employ many laundry workers, albeit fewer laundry workers than nurses. These workers are also employed by the many commercial laundries in Indianapolis and by institutions other than hospitals which operate their own laundries. Laundry workers are semiskilled. They may receive several weeks of on-the-job training, but there are no significant education or experience requirements for the position.

While unionization attempts have sporadically occurred in the past, none of the Indianapolis hospitals is now unionized. Except for supervisory personnel, the hospitals do not have long-term contracts with any employee groups. The seven large Indianapolis hospitals consult with each other about wage scales, but they do not bargain as a single unit with any employee group. Wage scales in the seven hospitals are usually similar, although each hospital has at times raised wages in an attempt to attract personnel from other hospitals.

The large Indianapolis hospitals maintain that there is a shortage of nurses. Each states that it cannot hire as many nurses as it would like at the current wage. Yet upon query each indicates that it would not be willing to raise wages to attract more nurses since it would lose money by doing so. In contrast, the hospitals feel that there are sufficient laundry workers. Each says that it can hire as many laundry workers as it desires at the present wage.

What, if anything, explains the seeming contradiction that hospitals cannot hire sufficient nurses at the present wage, but are unwilling to raise the wage to attract more nurses? Why doesn't this apparent contradiction also pertain to hospital employment of laundry workers?

6. A nationally affiliated union group coalesces among the practical nurses and nurses' aides at one of the large Indianapolis hospitals. After extensive discussions the hospital agrees to recognize the union, but on the condition that the arrangement be an open shop. That is, practical nurses or nurses' aides, either working at the hospital or later employed by the hospital, can join the union, but need not do so to retain or secure a position with the hospital. At the time of the agreement 60 percent of the hospital's practical nurses and nurses' aides belong to the union. Practical nurses and nurses' aides are not unionized at any other Indianapolis hospital.

Practical nurses have less education than do nurses, but still must complete organized training programs usually lasting one year. Nurses' aides receive informal on-the-job training from hospitals and other health care providers. As elsewhere, the nursing hierarchy in Indianapolis hospitals follows the relative skill levels of the three groups. Nurses occupy the top tier with practical nurses in between and nurses' aides at the bottom. The wage levels of the three groups are ordered in the same way, i.e., nurses are paid more than practical nurses who are paid more than nurses' aides. Reflecting their skill levels, the three types of personnel have distinctly different work patterns. Even so, there is considerable overlap in the kinds of work that the three personnel types can perform.

What will be the impact of the open shop agreement on the number of practical nurses and nurses' aides employed by the hospital? What will be its effect on the number of nurses employed?

7. After arduous negotiations another union succeeds in establishing a union shop for laundry workers at the seven large Indianapolis hospitals. Under the union shop arrangement laundry workers need not be union members to apply for and accept positions at the hospitals, but they must join the union within six weeks of employment. Similarly, current laundry workers must become union members within six weeks of the agreement. The new union then holds collective bargaining sessions with the hospitals. After several weeks an agreement is reached under which the wages of laundry workers are significantly increased.

What will be the impact of the new wage agreement on the following variables?

- number of laundry workers employed by the hospital;
- scope for discrimination by the hospital among laundry workers on the basis of race, sex, and/or other personal characteristics;
- extent of fringe benefits, such as free parking and reduced prices for meals provided by the hospital to laundry workers (such fringes are not covered by the union agreement);
- mechanization of laundry facilities by the hospital;
- development of contractual arrangements by the hospital to have its laundry processed by commercial laundries.

8. If the scenario described in the previous question applies not to laundry workers but rather to nurses (but not to practical nurses or nurses' aides), what will be the impact of the union wage agreement on the following variables?

- number of nurses employed by the hospital;
- scope for discrimination by the hospital among nurses on the basis of race, sex, and/or other personal characteristics;
- extent of fringe benefits offered by the hospital to nurses (as before, these fringes are not covered by the union agreement);
- number of practical nurses and nurses' aides employed by the hospital;
- number of practical nurses and nurses' aides employed by physician offices in Indianapolis.

DISCUSSION

1. The elderly are heavy consumers of hospital care. They are prone not only to acute severe illnesses, but also to chronic conditions which episodically require hospitalization. The Medicare program sharply reduced the price of hospital care to the elderly since it paid the great majority of the aged's hospitalization expenses. The quantity of hospital care demanded by the elderly therefore increased markedly. Put in another way, the Medicare program increased the elderly's effective demand for hospital services by placing additional dollars for such services at the elderly's command.

The demand for an input reflects the marginal revenue product of the input. The latter is defined as the marginal physical product of the input multiplied by the marginal revenue received by the firm for the additional output. If the market for the firm's products is perfectly competitive, the firm's marginal revenue for each output unit equals the market price of the unit. In that instance the marginal revenue product is termed the value marginal product.

In the technicians' case the Medicare program increased both their marginal product and the marginal revenue received by the hospital. The latter occurred because hospital prices rose sharply soon after the inception of the Medicare program due to the increased consumption of hospital care by the elderly. The former transpired because the Medicare-produced rise in the elderly's effective demand enabled technicians to increase their output. Since both the marginal revenue received by hospitals and the marginal physical product of technicians rose, hospital demand for these individuals increased.

This case illustrates two points. First, the demand for any input is a derived demand. It depends on the demand for the final product. The elderly do not demand X-ray or laboratory technicians, but rather hospital care which involves radiology and laboratory services.

Second, increasing the extent of insurance coverage can substantially change market conditions. The classic case for insurance is to protect against a loss so catastrophic that the presence of insurance does not alter the likelihood of the loss. For example, it is rare for people to kill themselves so that their survivors can collect the insurance proceeds. The threat of death is thus sufficient to make the insurance principle work well for life insurance.

However, the insurance principle is much less applicable to health insurance. Certain procedures (e.g., sigmoidoscopy) are sufficiently onerous and certain conditions (e.g., fractured hip) are sufficiently severe that the degree of insurance coverage has little impact on the type of care provided. However, for most conditions and procedures the reverse holds. That is, the physician, consumer, and/or hospital administrator have considerable discretion as to the type of care to be provided. Accordingly, when insurance coverage reduces the cost of health care to the consumer, it increases the consumer's effective demand for health services. At the same time insurance coverage lowers the cost consciousness of physicians and other providers, thereby further increasing demand.

The core of the difficulty is that the insurance principle presumes that the demand for the event insured against is perfectly price inelastic. As a consequence, reducing the price of the event through insurance does not influence the likelihood that the event will occur. The demand for certain health services is largely price inelastic, but the demand for most is not. Increasing the extent of health insurance therefore changes market conditions, as was graphically illustrated by the Medicare program.

2. For any individual increasing the wage has two effects. First, it increases the attractiveness of work compared to leisure because work now carries a higher rate of return. Second, it increases the individual's income since he or she can now work the same hours as before and still earn a higher income. The rise in income makes work less attractive compared to leisure since at least a major objective of work is to produce income which can be used for consumption. These two effects are termed respectively the substitution and income effects.

At low wage levels the substitution effect dominates the income effect, and the supply curve for the individual's labor is therefore upward sloping. However, as the wage increases and as the time worked rises, the income effect becomes progressively more important. Further, the increase in work time has two other effects. One is that the marginal value of leisure increases. As leisure time falls, the leisure opportunities forgone mount in value. The other is that the marginal value of work satisfaction declines. If an individual is working ten hours a week, he or she may enjoy working the eleventh hour, independent of the income produced. However, if the individual is working sixty hours a week, little psychic satisfaction is likely to result from working the sixty-first hour.

The consequence of these factors is that as the wage increases and as work time rises, work becomes valued progressively less compared to leisure. Eventually at high wage rates the supply curve of the individual's labor turns back on itself. That is, its slope is no longer positive, but rather negative. The result is the backward-bending supply curve of an individual's labor, which is depicted in Figure 10–1.

The supply curve of labor to an industry is the horizontal summation of the supply curves of those individuals either actually or potentially

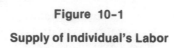

Figure 10-1

Supply of Individual's Labor

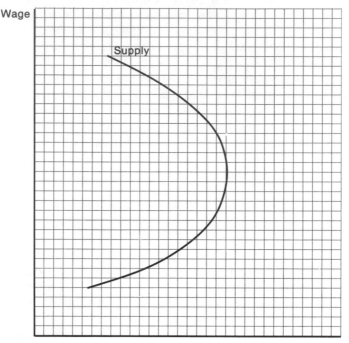

Individual's labor

working in the industry. The industry supply curve usually does not reach the backward bend within the relevant range. However, this may not be true if demand increases explosively and if labor resources cannot be readily transferred into the industry. Both conditions hold for radiologists. Demand has risen markedly during the last fifteen years. Supply cannot be expanded rapidly largely because of the long training period, but also because some of the factors increasing the demand for radiologists also raise the demand for other types of physicians.

The survey findings thus provide a logical explanation for the radiologist problems of Indianapolis hospitals. Compared to five years ago, radiologists are indeed working less and earning more per hour. The reason is that the sharp increase in demand and the constraints on supply have shifted the relevant range of the industry supply curve for radiologists to its backward-bending segment. This is illustrated in Figure 10-2. Five years ago the effective wage of radiologists was W_0 and the

Figure 10-2

Supply of Radiologists

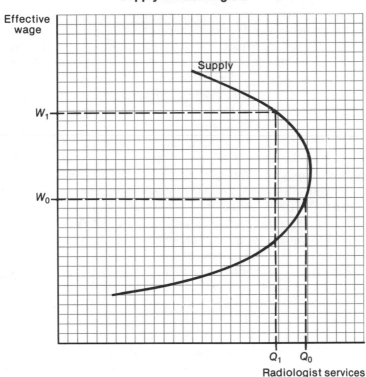

quantity of radiologist services was Q_0. Now the effective wage has risen substantially to W_1, but the quantity of services has fallen to Q_1.

If all Indianapolis hospitals acted together, they might be able to increase the supply of radiologist services by lowering their payments to these physicians. The difficulty is that if any hospital unilaterally takes this action, it is likely to find itself without even a bare minimum of radiologist services—a result which could gravely impair its ability to operate. Further, for a series of reasons, Indianapolis hospitals are unlikely to take concerted action against radiologists. First, radiologists have work opportunities outside hospitals; second, they can leave Indianapolis; third, physicians including radiologists are powerful decision makers within hospitals; and fourth, Indianapolis hospitals constitute a differentiated oligopoly with its conflicting mixture of collusive and competitive pressures.

3. Over a two-month period a hospital's demand for natural gas

147

will be highly price inelastic. Certain steps can be taken, such as reducing thermostats. However, major savings cannot be achieved in that length of time. In an institution as large as a hospital it may even be difficult in two months to set up an effective thermostat control system which balances heating costs and patient care requirements.

In contrast, substantial changes can be made during a two-year period. Insulation can be improved; heat retrieval systems can be developed; and the diverse departments of the hospital can be trained to conserve energy in different ways. It is even possible to select and then install a new heating system which would use a fuel other than natural gas, although such a change is likely to require more than two years.

A hospital's demand for natural gas is thus more price elastic over a two-year period than over a two-month period. It would be even more price elastic over a five-year period. The quantity of natural gas used by the hospital will thus be lower two years after the price increase than two months after the price rise.

These results are illustrated in Figure 10–3. D_0 and D_{10} are respectively the hospital's demand for natural gas over a two-month and a two-year period. Since the hospital cannot influence the price of natural gas and since no limits on availability have been imposed, the hospital's supply curve for natural gas is perfectly elastic at the market price within the relevant range. The hospital's initial supply curve is S_0 which reflects the original market price of P_0. At that price the hospital consumes Q_0 of natural gas. When the price rises to P_1, the supply curve becomes S_1. At the end of two months the quantity of natural gas consumed by the hospital is Q_1, while at the end of two years it is the distinctly lower Q_2.

4. Both hospitals and physician offices will reduce their use of these disposable items in response to the price increases. However, the reaction by hospitals will be much larger. Disposable items constitute an important expense category for hospitals, while their cost significance to physician offices is much lower. The hospital will therefore carefully consider possible reactions to the price increase, whereas many physician offices may find it cost-ineffective to even consider the matter.

The result is that the demand by hospitals for these disposable items is more price elastic than the demand by physician offices. The decline in the quantity purchased will thus be larger for hospitals than for physician offices. However, there may be certain physician offices, such as an allergy clinic, which extensively use the disposable items. If so, their response will more closely resemble that of hospitals.

The point made here holds generally. If an item represents only a minor expense for a firm, i.e., if its relative importance to the firm is low, the firm's demand for the item will be price inelastic. This relation-

Figure 10-3

Demand for Natural Gas

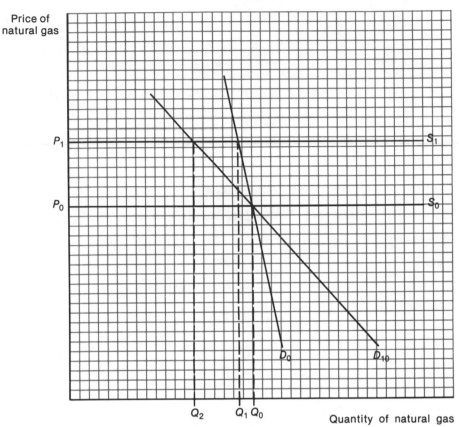

ship is analogous to the one between the elasticity of product demand and the percentage of the consumer's income spent on the product. The rationale underlying the relationship is the same in each case. If a firm or an individual buys only three widgets a year, it is immaterial whether each widget costs $.50 or $1.00.

5. Since laundry workers are semiskilled, their wage will be largely set by the prevailing wages of semiskilled workers in the Indianapolis market. Even more important, hospitals are only a small component of the Indianapolis market for laundry workers. As a consequence, hospitals cannot appreciably influence the wage of laundry workers. That is, they can employ as many laundry workers as they desire at the prevailing

149

wage, but they will be unable to hire any such workers if they offer less than that wage.

The overall market for laundry workers in Indianapolis may or may not approximate perfect competition. It is likely that it does because there are many firms in the market and because laundry workers are semiskilled. However, from the hospital's standpoint it is a perfectly competitive labor market. Each hospital faces a perfectly elastic supply curve at the prevailing market wage for laundry workers.

This situation is illustrated for a representative hospital in Figure 10-4. The hospital pays laundry workers a wage of W_0. At that wage the hospital employs N_0 quantity of laundry workers. At wage W_0 the quantity of laundry workers demanded by the hospital equals the

Figure 10-4

Hospital's Demand for Laundry Workers

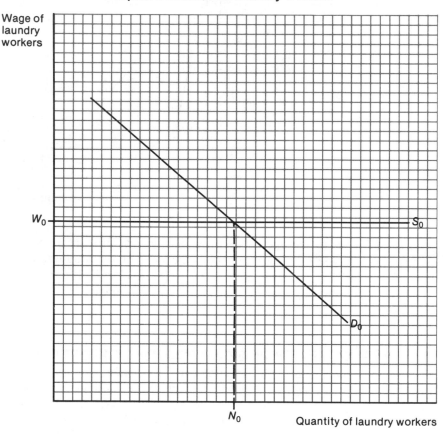

quantity supplied. The hospital thus does not feel that there is a shortage of laundry workers.

In contrast to laundry workers, nurses are skilled workers specialized to the health care field. The seven hospitals together are by far the largest employer of nurses in the Indianapolis area. Each hospital alone is sufficiently large that to attract more nurses it must pay a higher wage. That is, each hospital faces an upward-sloping supply curve for nurses.

This situation is termed oligopsony. It is the analogue in the input market for oligopoly in the product market. If there were only a single buyer of nurses' services in the Indianapolis area, the situation would then be termed monopsony. While oligopoly and oligopsony are usually defined in terms of the product and input markets respectively, both may exist in the same market. That is, a small number of buyers may face a small number of sellers. If this situation holds, it is termed a bilateral oligopoly. If there is only a single seller and a single buyer, the situation is then termed a bilateral monopoly.

The oligopsonist's situation is depicted in Figure 10-5. The hospital faces an upward-sloping supply curve for nurses, S_0; its demand for nurses is D_0. In terms of using inputs, Indianapolis hospitals act sufficiently like profit maximizers that they will set marginal revenue equal to marginal cost. The demand curve indicates the revenue that the hospital will gain by employing additional nurses. That is, it indicates the marginal revenue produced by each nurse.

Since the supply curve is upward sloping, the marginal cost of employing a nurse does not equal the wage. To attract an additional nurse the hospital must pay a higher wage. However, since it pays all nurses the same wage, the hospital must then pay the higher wage to the nurses hired previously at the lower wage. The hospital's marginal cost of nurses therefore equals the wage plus the wage increment paid to the nurses employed previously.

The oligopsonist's marginal cost is thus analogous to the oligopolist's marginal revenue. Since the supply curve is a straight line, the marginal cost curve is also a straight line. As shown in Figure 10-5, its positive slope is twice that of the supply curve and it intersects the wage axis at the same point as the supply curve.

To determine how many nurses to employ, the hospital equates marginal revenue with marginal cost. This occurs at the intersection of the demand and marginal cost curves. The hospital will thus employ N_0 nurses. To attract that number of nurses the hospital pays a wage of W_0. However, at that wage the hospital would be willing to hire N_1 nurses if it did not have to raise the wage to do so.

Thus arises the paradox of the oligopsonist. The hospital perceives that there is a shortage of nurses. That is, it cannot hire as many nurses

Figure 10-5

Hospital's Demand for Nurses

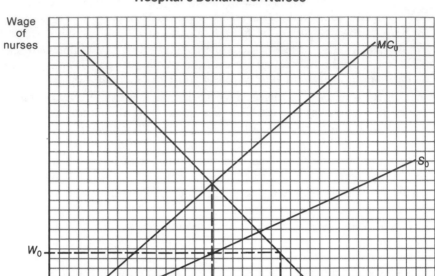

as it would like at the current wage. However, the hospital will not increase the wage to attract more nurses since the marginal cost of this action exceeds its marginal revenue.

Earlier in the discussion the point was made that regardless of whether the overall laundry worker market is perfectly competitive, the hospital acts like a perfect competitor in that market. A similar point holds in the market for nurses. Each of the seven large hospitals is an oligopsonist in this market, but many nursing homes and most physician offices act like perfect competitors. Because of their small size they can hire as many nurses as they like at the prevailing market wage. That is, within their relevant range they face a perfectly elastic supply curve for nurses.

Many labor markets display this heterogeneity. That is, there are some firms sufficiently large that they act like oligopsonists and other firms sufficiently small that they act like perfect competitors. The analogous point is true of many product markets. However, in either case increasing differentiation will reduce the number of perfect competitors. For example, a small hospital specializing in gastrointestinal diseases will prefer to hire nurses with experience in this area. It will thus face a steeper supply curve for nurses than will a similar-sized general hospital.

6. There is a large pool of practical nurses and nurses' aides in the Indianapolis area. To work at the hospital, a practical nurse or nurses' aide need not belong to the union. In fact, only 60 percent of the practical nurses and nurses' aides who are currently employed are union members. Therefore, if the union exerts meaningful wage pressure on the hospital, the hospital will simply shift to nonunion employees. The open shop agreement will thus not have a significant impact on the number of practical nurses and nurses' aides employed by the hospital. Nor will it have an appreciable effect on the quantity of nurses employed.

This question illustrates the futility of open shops. It also makes it clear why unions have steadfastly opposed state "right-to work" laws which require open shops, and the federal Taft-Hartley Act which permits states to have such laws. Although an ineffective instrument for raising wages, open shops can be useful at times as a tactical device. That is, as an initial step the union can gain recognition as an open shop and then later move on to tighter arrangements.

7. The situation of a representative hospital is shown in Figure 10–6. Initially the hospital faced a perfectly elastic supply curve at wage W_0. After the union agreement it still faces a perfectly elastic supply curve but at the higher wage, W_1. The hospital will therefore reduce the number of laundry workers employed from N_0 to N_1.

Since the hospitals are small relative to the Indianapolis market for laundry workers, the unionization agreement will not affect the wage prevailing in that market. It will still be W_0. Since hospitals are paying laundry workers a wage higher than the market wage, many more laundry workers will be willing to work for hospitals than hospitals will be willing to employ at the wage W_1. That is, after the union agreement there will be a large excess supply of laundry workers in the hospital market. Hospitals will thus be able to select their laundry workers from among many candidates. That being the case, there will be greater scope for discrimination of all types, including that based on race or sex.

Under the union agreement the hospital is paying a higher wage to laundry workers than it would prefer. Further, the union wage is higher

153

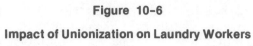

Figure 10-6

Impact of Unionization on Laundry Workers

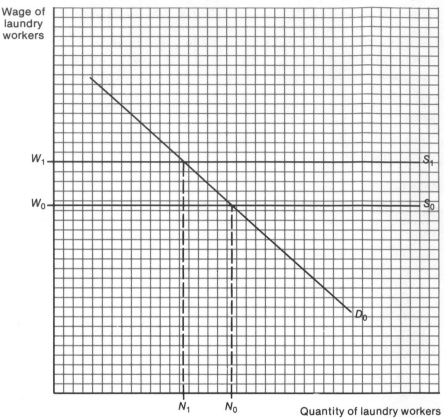

than the prevailing market wage for laundry workers in Indianapolis. The situation is thus conducive to wage shading, which is analogous to price shading, albeit the term is used less frequently. The hospital will practice wage shading by reducing the fringe benefits not covered by the union agreement. By doing so the hospital will achieve a desired objective: it will decrease the effective wage of laundry workers. On the other side, laundry workers will be willing to accept the lower fringe benefits because the wage itself is higher than that they can obtain elsewhere.

While wage shading will reduce the impact of the union wage increase, its extent is unlikely to be sufficient to restore the situation to the pre-union equilibrium. Laundry workers will thus be higher-priced inputs to the hospital after the agreement than they were before. Since capital and labor are partial substitutes in processing laundry and since labor is now higher priced, the hospital will seriously consider increasing the mechanization of its laundry facilities and may take steps in this direction.

Another alternative, which is used by many hospitals independent of unionization, is to have laundry processed outside the hospital by a commercial firm. This alternative will now be more attractive to the hospital than it was previously since the union agreement will not affect the wages paid by commercial laundries. The hospital will therefore now be more likely than before to conclude a contractual arrangement under which its laundry is processed by an outside firm.

8. This situation is presented in Figure 10–7. Before unionization the demand, supply, and marginal cost curves are respectively D_0, S_0, and MC_0. W_1 is the wage established by the union agreement. Accordingly, the hospital can now employ at a wage of W_1 as many nurses as it desires up to N_2 nurses. Beyond that quantity the hospital must once again raise the wage in order to attract more nurses. The postunion supply curve, S_1, is therefore perfectly elastic at wage W_1 from zero to N_2 nurses, and identical to the previous supply curve above N_2 nurses.

Since the hospital need not raise the wage to hire more nurses until it employs more than N_2 nurses, the postunion marginal cost curve, MC_1, is perfectly elastic at wage W_1 from zero to N_2 nurses. Above that quantity of nurses the hospital must once again increase the wage to hire more nurses. Since the preunion and postunion supply curves are identical above N_2 nurses, so are the marginal cost curves.

As before the hospital will equate marginal revenue with marginal cost in order to determine how many nurses to employ. After the agreement the marginal cost curve intersects the demand curve at N_1 nurses. The agreement thus increases the number of nurses employed by the hospital from N_0 to N_1.

At the new wage W_1, N_2 number of nurses are willing to work but the hospital will only employ N_1 nurses. Excess supply thus exists at the wage W_1. In the postunion situation there is thus increased scope for discrimination by the hospital among nurses on the basis of race, sex, and other personal characteristics. However, the discrimination effect is smaller in this situation than in the laundry worker case since in the latter a larger difference exists between the number of employees hired by the hospital and the number willing to work at the union wage.

After unionization the hospital employs N_1 nurses at a wage of W_1, but that number of nurses is willing to work at a wage of W_2. Wage shading will therefore occur with the hospital reducing the fringe benefits offered to nurses. However, as with the discrimination effect and for

155

Figure 10-7

Impact of Unionization on Nurses

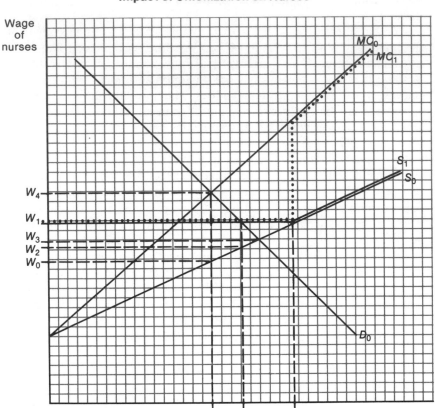

similar reasons, wage shading will not be as great here as in the laundry worker case.

Because the seven hospitals are large relative to the market for nurses, the union agreement will increase the prevailing wage for nurses in the Indianapolis market. Physician offices will therefore shift away from nurses and toward substitutes, such as practical nurses and nurses' aides. A side effect of the agreement will therefore be an increase in the number of practical nurses and nurses' aides employed by physician offices.

The impact of the union agreement on the number of practical nurses/nurses' aides employed by the hospital is less straightforward. The wage of nurses will be higher, but so will the number employed. As a result of the latter, the number of practical nurses/nurses' aides used by the

156

hospital is likely to decrease. However, the hospital will also react to the increased wage of nurses by increasing the efficiency with which it uses its now higher-priced input. This process could soften the reduction in the number of practical nurses/nurses' aides and could even lead to an increase in their employment.

Unlike the laundry worker case, the results here depend critically on the extent to which the wage is raised. If the union wage is less than W_3, the number of nurses employed will increase, but there will be no wage shading and no increased scope for discrimination. If the union wage is between W_3 and W_4, the results will be those described above with the relative magnitude of the effects depending upon whether the wage approaches W_3 or W_4. Finally, if the union wage is above W_4, the number of nurses employed will not increase but rather decrease; the degree of wage shading will be substantial; and the scope for discrimination will be large.

The impact of unionization depends on a number of factors, but paramount among these is the structure of the specific labor market, as pointed up by the nurse and laundry worker cases. If the labor market is competitive, the effects of unionization will be mixed. The union may increase the wage, but the number employed will fall as a result. In addition, the wage increase may significantly encourage discrimination and may be partially offset by extensive wage shading. However, if the market is oligopsonistic, the effects of unionization may be largely beneficial at least from the standpoint of labor. In this setting a union-engineered increase in the wage may in fact increase the number employed. It may also have little effect on discrimination and may only modestly encourage wage shading. When evaluating unionization, it is therefore essential to examine carefully the nature of the labor market involved—a step often neglected by advocates on both sides of union issues.

Important Concepts

Time as a Productive Resource
Interest Rate
Present Value
Discount Rate
Maximization of Present Value of Profit
Production Function
Law of Diminishing Returns
Marginal Physical Product
Average Physical Product
Technical Maximum
Risk of Loss
Probability
Expected Profit
Risk Preference
Multiple Products
Competition Between Multiple Products
Complementarity Between Multiple Products
Product Quality
Economic Life of Forest

11
Cultivation
of Douglas Fir

The Pervasive Influence
of Time

An important inhabitant of western forests is the Douglas fir, a coniferous tree also known as the Puget Sound spruce and Oregon pine. Grown commercially along the West Coast from central British Columbia to northern Mexico, the Douglas fir is a major source of lumber in North America. Although not as large as the Redwood, it can still attain a height of more than three hundred feet and a girth of more than six feet. A stand of Douglas fir does not usually reach its maximum yield until about its 150th year, i.e., more than twice as long as the biblical three score and ten.

Table 11−1 depicts the commercial production of a stand of Douglas fir. Located in a remote area of western Oregon, the stand is owned by the Lupine Lumber Company, a profit-maximizing firm. The table is stated in terms of the growth per acre that will occur after an area has been logged and then reseeded. It assumes that the trees will receive routine care at appropriate intervals based on accepted forestry techniques. However, the table also assumes that the intensity of this care will be low and that the main factor contributing to the forest's growth will be the natural environment, i.e., the land and the climate.

1. Complete Table 11−1. Does the Douglas fir production function shown in the table conform to the law of diminishing returns?

2. As is evident in Table 11−1, the production of Douglas fir requires time. It is therefore necessary to consider the real rate of interest, which is defined as the market rate of interest adjusted to remove the effects of general price inflation. For ease of exposition, in this book this variable will be referred to simply as the interest rate. Explain why the descriptive

Table 11-1

Production Function for Douglas Fir

Year of Growth	Total Growth	Growth During Previous Decade	Average Growth Per Decade
20th	1,250 cu. ft.		
30	3,300		
40	5,250		
50	7,100		
60	8,700		
70	10,150		
80	11,350		
90	12,390		
100	13,270		
110	14,000		
120	14,600		
130	15,140		
140	15,610		
150	16,060		
160	16,490		
170	16,300		
180	16,060		
190	15,780		

phrase—the price of time—has sometimes been applied to the interest rate.

3. A definitive way to assess the influence of time is to determine the present value of revenue that will be earned in the future. Present value is defined as the value today of a specific asset or a particular income stream in the future. The present value of a future liability or cost is defined analogously. Illustrating the present value concept, if the interest rate is 5 percent, $105 one year from today has the same value as $100 today. The present value of $105 one year in the future is thus $100.

The present value of revenue received at a specific point in the future is determined by the formula shown below.

$$PV_R = \frac{R}{(1 + i)^t}$$

Where PV_R = present value of R revenue in the tth year;
    R = revenue in the tth year;
    i = interest rate; and
    t = tth year.

To eliminate the need for repeated and laborious calculations, present value tables have been prepared and are used widely. Such a table is displayed in Table 11–2. It includes four interest rates: 1 percent, 3 percent, 5 percent, and 10 percent. In addition to the fifth and tenth years, all the years in Table 11–1 are contained in this table.

The interest rate is sometimes referred to as the discount rate. Does Table 11–2 illustrate this concept? If so, what is being discounted?

4. The stand of Douglas fir owned by the Lupine Lumber Company attains its maximum growth in its 160th year. Should Lupine harvest the timber in this year?

5. The price of Douglas fir is $3 per cubic foot and the harvesting cost is $.80 per cubic foot. Both these values are expected to prevail into the indefinite future. Presume throughout this chapter that Lupine can invest the proceeds gained by harvesting the Douglas fir in various opportunities which pay the rate of interest prevailing in the economy. However, for the sake of simplicity, assume that Lupine cannot reinvest these proceeds in this stand of Douglas fir by reseeding the land after the timber is harvested.

If the prevailing rate of interest is 3 percent when will Lupine crop the Douglas fir? If the interest rate is instead 5 percent, when will the Douglas fir be harvested?

6. The interest rate is now expected to remain 3 percent indefinitely. Harvesting cost is still $.80 per cubic foot, but the price of Douglas fir is now $4.50 per cubic foot—a level which is expected to continue indefinitely. When will Lupine now harvest the Douglas fir?

7. The interest rate and the price of Douglas fir are now expected to remain indefinitely at 3 percent and $3 per cubic foot respectively. However, harvesting cost is now expected to be $1.20 per cubic foot and to

Table 11–2

Present Value of One Dollar

Year Dollar Received	Present Value at Different Interest Rates			
	1%	3%	5%	10%
5th	0.95	0.86	0.78	0.62
10	0.91	0.74	0.61	0.39
20	0.82	0.55	0.38	0.15
30	0.74	0.41	0.23	0.06
40	0.67	0.31	0.14	0.02
50	0.61	0.23	0.09	0.01
60	0.55	0.17	0.05	0.00
70	0.50	0.13	0.03	0.00
80	0.45	0.09	0.02	0.00
90	0.41	0.07	0.01	0.00
100	0.37	0.05	0.01	0.00
110	0.33	0.04	0.00	0.00
120	0.30	0.03	0.00	0.00
130	0.27	0.02	0.00	0.00
140	0.25	0.02	0.00	0.00
150	0.22	0.01	0.00	0.00
160	0.20	0.01	0.00	0.00
170	0.18	0.01	0.00	0.00
180	0.17	0.00	0.00	0.00
190	0.15	0.00	0.00	0.00

continue at that level in the future. In what year will the Oregon company now crop the Douglas fir?

8. The production function shown in Table 11–1 reflects the usual damage done by disease and insects. However, it does not take into account the risk of total destruction by fire. This risk is presented in Table 11−3, which indicates the probability of total fire loss by the time of the respective year. For example, the probability is .024 that the Douglas fir will be totally destroyed by fire either before or in the 60th year. That is, there is a 2.4 percent chance that such fire destruction will occur.

In this situation the interest rate, price, and harvesting cost are expected to remain indefinitely 3 percent, $3 per cubic foot, and $.80

Table 11−3

Fire Loss

Year of Growth	Probability of Total Loss
20th	.006
30	.010
40	.014
50	.019
60	.024
70	.030
80	.037
90	.043
100	.049
110	.054
120	.059
130	.064
140	.069
150	.074
160	.079
170	.084
180	.089
190	.094

per cubic foot. Faced with the risk of fire loss, when will Lupine harvest the Douglas fir?

9. As a Douglas fir forest matures, it becomes a valuable recreation area for activities such as backpacking, fishing, and hunting. At times timber companies can earn profits from such recreational use. Assume that this is now the case for the stand of Douglas fir and that the present values of recreational profits are those displayed in Table 11–4.

The interest rate, price of Douglas fir, and harvesting cost are still expected to remain the same values as in the previous question, but there is now no risk of fire loss. In this situation when will the Oregon company crop the Douglas fir?

Table 11–4

Profits from Recreational Use

Year of Growth	Present Value of Recreational Profit
20th	$ 544
30	1,128
40	1,968
50	2,681
60	3,200
70	3,613
80	3,793
90	3,936

10. In actuality, the value of Douglas fir as lumber increases as the trees become larger with age. Reflecting this point, assume that Douglas fir prices are those shown in Table 11–5 and that these prices are expected to continue indefinitely.

The interest rate and harvesting cost are expected to continue at 3 percent and $.80 per cubic foot respectively. In this situation there is no risk of fire and no possibility of recreational profits. When will Lupine now harvest the Douglas fir?

Table 11-5

Increase in Timber Value

Age of Wood	Price
20 yrs.	$1.60
30	2.00
40	2.40
50	2.90
60	3.50
70	4.10
80	4.60
90 and beyond	5.00

11. Now consider briefly another change in timber prices. In the United States there is increasing demand for land of many types; the trend in real income remains upward. It is thus not unreasonable to postulate that in the future lumber prices will increase relative to other prices. If this occurs, what will be the impact on Lupine's harvest year?

DISCUSSION

1. Table 11–6 displays the Douglas fir production function, which is stated on a per-acre basis. The first two columns in the table are the same as those in Table 11–1. The third and fourth columns depict respectively the growth during the previous decade and the average growth per decade. The former is the marginal physical product of time and the latter the average physical product of time.

The marginal physical product equals the total growth present in the year in question minus the total growth present ten years earlier. The average physical product is defined as the total growth present in the year in question divided by the decades of growth. As examples, the marginal product at the 30th year equals the total growth by that year minus the total growth by the 20th year, or 3,300 cubic feet minus 1,250 cubic feet, or 2,050 cubic feet. The average product at the 30th year

165

equals the total growth by that year divided by the number of decades, or 3,300 cubic feet divided by 3, or 1,100 cubic feet per decade.

The law of diminishing returns has most frequently been applied to production at a point in time, especially to increasing the number of farmers working a fixed plot of land. However, the law holds equally well in this situation. The production function in Table 11–6 presumes

Table 11–6

Production Function for Douglas Fir

Year of Growth	Total Growth	Growth During Previous Decade	Average Growth Per Decade
20th	1,250 cu. ft.	——	625 cu. ft.
30	3,300	2,050 cu. ft.	1,100
40	5,250	1,950	1,313
50	7,100	1,850	1,420
60	8,700	1,600	1,450
70	10,150	1,450	1,450
80	11,350	1,200	1,419
90	12,390	1,040	1,377
100	13,270	880	1,327
110	14,000	730	1,273
120	14,600	600	1,217
130	15,140	540	1,165
140	15,610	470	1,115
150	16,060	450	1,071
160	16,490	430	1,031
170	16,300	– 190	959
180	16,060	– 240	892
190	15,780	– 280	831

that at least two inputs will remain unchanged—the land and climate. It also assumes no significant technological changes will occur. The variable input is time. As the forest is allowed to grow and mature, increasing amounts of time are used to produce Douglas fir.

The results conform to the law of diminishing returns. From the 30th year onward the marginal product of time gradually diminishes. The forest reaches its maximum yield in its 160th year. After that point the marginal product of time not only decreases, but is also negative. That is, the stage of absolutely decreasing returns has been reached. The earlier stage of increasing returns is also evident in Table 11–6, albeit not as explicitly. The marginal product of time during the third decade is 2,050 cubic feet, which exceeds the total product at the end of the second decade.

The behavior of the average product is also consistent with the law of diminishing returns, as it must be given the relationships between the average and marginal products. Average product rapidly increases during the early years of forest growth, reaching a maximum in the 60th and 70th years. In the latter year the average and marginal products are equal. After that time average product declines but more gradually than marginal product, so that the difference between the two becomes progressively greater.

2. Time has value. As in the case of Douglas fir, it is a critical input in many productive processes. Further, time is scarce, at least in terms of production in the current world. That is, limitless quantities are not available. Like other valuable and scarce resources, time carries a price. It indicates the prevailing trade-offs between the present and future use of a product or resource. This price is the interest rate.

Illustrating this point, if the interest rate is 4 percent, a firm can borrow resources which it can use now, but only if it pays an annual price equal to 4 percent of the resources' value. Conversely, a firm can earn an annual return of 4 percent by allowing others to use its resources. The first firm is willing to pay the 4 percent price to the second firm since it can use the resources to make products which are valuable. If the first firm did not borrow the resources, it would be giving up the opportunity of producing additional output during the present time period. Since this opportunity has value, the price of time, i.e., the interest rate, is positive.

So far the discussion has been framed in terms of production. Production alone is sufficient to place a positive price on time. However, the price of time is also positive from a consumption standpoint. Not only does the consumer face ultimate death, but he or she lives in a world of uncertainty. Premature death and disability can occur; adverse events of

167

a less calamitous nature happen frequently. Faced with this situation, the individual will prefer present consumption to future consumption. That is, he or she will not be willing to defer consumption from the present to the future unless there is some compensation. Conversely, an individual is willing to pay a price to consume now rather than in the future.

3. As discussed above, the interest rate is the price of time. As this rate increases, time becomes progressively more expensive. In other words, as the interest rate rises, the value of the future in terms of the present declines. That is, the future is progressively discounted as the interest rate increases. It is thus appropriate to refer to the interest rate as the discount rate.

These points are well illustrated in Table 11–2. Consider the present value at different interest rates of $1 received in the 20th year. If the interest rate is 1 percent, that $1 has a present value of $.82. That is, $1 in the 20th year is equivalent to $.82 today. If the interest rate rises to 3 or 5 percent, the present value of the $1 in the 20th year declines to $.55 or $.38 respectively. If the interest rate is as high as 10 percent, the $1 in the 20th year is worth only $.15 today, i.e., far lower than the present value of $.82 when the interest rate is 1 percent.

4. During the sixteenth decade the marginal product of time is very low, equaling 430 cubic feet. In percentage terms the marginal product is also low, with the average annual growth rate during this decade approximating .3 percent, i.e., 430 cubic feet divided by 16,060 cubic feet divided by 10 years. It will therefore only be profitable for Lupine to retain the trees through their 160th year in highly unusual circumstances, such as a very low rate of interest or a dramatic increase in the quality of the timber during the sixteenth decade. In all ordinary situations Lupine should harvest the trees much earlier than their 160th year.

The 160th year when total growth reaches its highest point is an example of a technical maximum. By definition the marginal product of some input must be approaching zero at a technical maximum. If this were not the case, output would not peak but rather would continue to increase. As long as the prices of all inputs are significantly positive, it will not be profitable to produce at a technical maximum.

While this conclusion may seem counterintuitive, it is not since the input whose marginal product is low can be used more advantageously in other pursuits. Illustrating this point, very little lumber is gained by leaving the resources in the timber from the 150th to the 160th year. Substantially more output can be attained by shifting the resources from this stand of timber to other uses.

5. Since the production of Douglas fir requires many years, it is necessary to explicitly take into account the influence of time in order to determine the profit-maximizing output. Consonant with the earlier discussions in this chapter, it would be grossly inaccurate, for example, to compare profits in the 100th and 30th years, and to then harvest in the 100th year since profits in that year are higher. Rather, profits in future years must be discounted back to the present, since the Douglas fir should be harvested when the present value of profit reaches its highest value. That is, Lupine should maximize the present value of profit, rather than simply profit.

This situation is presented in Table 11–7. The first column in the table indicates the years of growth pertinent to this case. The second, third and fourth columns show respectively total revenue, harvesting cost, and profit attained in each year. Total revenue equals the price of $3 per cubic foot multiplied by the total growth present in each year. Harvesting cost is analogous; it equals the product of total growth and the per unit cost of $.80 per cubic foot. Profit equals the difference between total revenue and harvesting cost.

The influence of time is incorporated in the fifth and sixth table columns. The former shows the present value of profit when the interest rate is 3 percent, while the latter indicates the present value when the

Table 11-7

Impact of Interest Rate Increase

Year of Growth	Total Revenue	Harvesting Cost	Profit	Present Value of Profit	
				Interest Rate at 3%	Interest Rate at 5%
20th	$ 3,750	$1,000	$ 2,750	$1,513	$1,045
30	9,900	2,640	7,260	2,977	1,670
40	15,750	4,200	11,550	3,581	1,617
50	21,300	5,680	15,620	3,593	1,406
60	26,100	6,960	19,140	3,254	957
70	30,450	8,120	22,330	2,903	670
80	34,050	9,080	24,970	2,247	499
90	37,170	9,912	27,258	1,908	273

interest rate is 5 percent. Each is calculated by multiplying profit in the year in question by the corresponding discount factor shown in Table 11-2. For example, the present value of profit in the 40th year at a 3 percent interest rate is $3,581, which is the product of that year's profit ($11,550) and the appropriate discount factor (.31).

As shown in the table, if the interest rate is 3 percent, Lupine will harvest in the 50th year when the present value of profit attains its maximum level of $3,593. However, if the interest rate is 5 percent, the present value of profit peaks in the 30th year, when it equals $1,670. The Oregon firm will therefore harvest in that year if a 5 percent interest rate prevails.

The increase in the interest rate from 3 to 5 percent substantially reduces the economic life of the forest from fifty years to thirty years. This impact is consistent with the earlier discussions. As the interest rate rises, time becomes more expensive. As a consequence, less time should be devoted to the production of Douglas fir.

6. This situation is analyzed in Table 11-8. The first two columns are drawn from previous tables. The third column shows the net price of Douglas fir, which is defined as the gross price of $4.50 per cubic foot minus the harvesting cost of $.80 per cubic foot. Profit, shown in the fourth column, equals total growth multiplied by net price. The fifth

Table 11-8

Impact of Price Increase

Year of Growth	Total Growth	Net Price	Profit	Present Value of Profit
20th	1,250 cu. ft.	$3.70	$ 4,625	$2,544
30	3,300	3.70	12,210	5,006
40	5,250	3.70	19,425	6,022
50	7,100	3.70	26,270	6,042
60	8,700	3.70	32,190	5,472
70	10,150	3.70	37,555	4,882
80	11,350	3.70	41,995	3,780
90	12,390	3.70	45,843	3,209

column indicates the present value of profit; it is calculated as in Table 11−7.

Perhaps somewhat surprisingly, the price increase does not alter the optimal harvest time. It remains the 50th year. The reason is that while the price rise makes the timber more valuable in all years, it does not change the timber's value in one year compared to other years. For example, thirty-year wood and sixty-year wood are still equally valuable, i.e., each carries a price of $4.50 per cubic foot. Therefore, while profits will now be much higher in the 50th year than they were previously, the amount of time invested in the trees should not change. The Douglas fir should still be grown by Lupine for 50 years.

7. As displayed in Table 11−9, this situation is analogous to the price increase discussed earlier. The increased harvesting costs diminish profit in each year, but they do not alter the optimal harvest year. Lupine will therefore still crop the Douglas fir in the 50th year.

8. If no fire loss occurs, profit will be the same as it was previously. This figure is displayed in the second column of Table 11−10. However, there is now a small but appreciable risk that the Douglas fir will be totally destroyed by fire. Correspondingly, there is a probability that there will be no fire loss. It equals 1.000 minus the probability of total

Table 11-9

Impact of Harvesting Cost Increase

Year of Growth	Total Growth	Net Price	Profit	Present Value of Profit
20th	1,250 cu. ft.	$1.80	$ 2,250	$1,237
30	3,300	1.80	5,940	2,435
40	5,250	1.80	9,450	2,929
50	7,100	1.80	12,780	2,939
60	8,700	1.80	15,660	2,662
70	10,150	1.80	18,270	2,375
80	11,350	1.80	20,430	1,839
90	12,390	1.80	22,302	1,561

Table 11-10

Impact of Fire Risk

Year of Growth	Profit Without Fire Loss	Probability of No Fire Loss	Expected Profit	Present Value of Expected Profit
20th	$ 2,750	.994	$ 2,733	$1,503
30	7,260	.990	7,187	2,947
40	11,550	.986	11,388	3,530
50	15,620	.981	15,323	3,524
60	19,140	.976	18,681	3,176
70	22,330	.970	21,660	2,816
80	24,970	.963	24,046	2,164
90	27,258	.957	26,086	1,826

fire destruction, which is shown in Table 11-3. This probability is indicated in the third column of Table 11-10.

In this situation Lupine cannot simply maximize the present value of profits, assuming that there will be no fire destruction. Rather, it must maximize the present value of expected profits, which equals profit in the absence of fire destruction multiplied by the probability that fire destruction will not occur. Expected profit and the present value of this profit are presented in the fourth and fifth columns respectively of Table 11-10.

The optimal harvest time is now the 40th year. The risk of fire loss thus reduces the optimal logging time by a decade. The reason is that the additional profits gained during the fifth decade are not sufficient to offset the risk that all profits may be lost through fire destruction.

Like many risks, fire loss is an either/or situation. For example, profit in the 40th year will not equal $11,388. It will either be $11,550 or zero. Since the risk of loss is low, the expected profit is only slightly less than the profit in the absence of loss.

Even so, it is important to note the divergent nature of the two outcomes. The analysis in Table 11-10 implicitly assumes that Lupine is neutral in terms of risk preference. That is, to determine expected profit the Oregon company simply multiplies the profit in the absence of loss times the probability that there will be no loss. However, there may be firms highly adverse to risk which are not willing to do this. They may wish to impose additional constraints to reduce the risk of total loss, with the result that the timber may be cropped in an earlier year. Similarly, risk-taking firms may be willing to delay the harvesting of the Douglas fir until the 50th year.

9. The forest now produces two products—timber and recreation. In any multiple product situation the firm should maximize total profits, rather than the profits of either product. This principle applies here. That is, to determine the optimal harvest year it is necessary to add the present value of recreational profit to the present value of timber profit in order to obtain the present value of total profit.

This procedure is carried out in Table 11–11. The present value of timber profit and the present value of recreational profit are drawn respectively from Tables 11–7 and 11–4. The latter steadily increases, rising from $544 in the 20th year to $3,936 in the 90th year. In contrast, and as analyzed previously, the present value of timber profit increases from the 20th year through the 50th year and then declines through the 90th year. The net result is that the present value of total profit reaches a maximum in the 70th year. The addition of the recreational income

Table 11-11

Impact of Recreational Use

Year of Growth	Present Value of Timber Profit	Present Value of Recreational Profit	Present Value of Total Profit
20th	$1,513	$ 544	$2,057
30	2,977	1,128	4,105
40	3,581	1,968	5,549
50	3,593	2,681	6,274
60	3,254	3,200	6,454
70	2,903	3,613	6,516
80	2,247	3,793	6,040
90	1,908	3,936	5,844

stream thus extends the economically useful life of the forest by two decades.

Multiple products of the same productive process can at times be complementary and at other times competitive. Both characteristics are illustrated by this situation. Through the forest's 50th year the timber and recreational uses are complementary. The present value of each activity's profit increases during the forest's first five decades. After that time the timber and recreational uses become competitive. The present value of timber profit declines while the present value of recreational profit continues to rise. Initially the latter outweighs the former, but after the 70th year the reverse is true. The forest should therefore be harvested by Lupine in that year.

10. This situation is analyzed in Table 11–12, whose columns are analogous to those of Tables 11–8 and 11–9. As indicated, the present value of profit now reaches its maximum level in the 70th year. The change in the price structure thus increases the economic life of the forest by two decades.

This case illustrates the impact of product quality on decision making. In earlier questions the wood did not increase in value as the trees matured. Now this is no longer true. As the forest matures, not only is

Table 11–12

Impact of Increasing Timber Value

Year of Growth	Total Growth	Net Price	Profit	Present Value of Profit
20th	1,250 cu. ft.	$ .80	$ 1,000	$ 550
30	3,300	1.20	3,960	1,624
40	5,250	1.60	8,400	2,604
50	7,100	2.10	14,910	3,429
60	8,700	2.70	23,490	3,993
70	10,150	3.30	33,495	4,354
80	11,350	3.80	43,130	3,882
90	12,390	4.20	52,038	3,643

additional quantity obtained, but also additional quality. It is therefore profitable for Lupine to invest an additional two decades of time in Douglas fir production.

11. While the origin of this pricing change differs from that discussed above, the general effect is similar. In each instance the value of timber rises as the duration of growth increases. An expected relative increase in lumber prices in the future will thus extend the economic life of the forest.

This might not be true if Lupine's stand of Douglas fir were located near a populated area, since in that case the rising demand for land for nonlumber purposes might lead to earlier harvesting. The same would apply if Lupine's stand were situated near a recreational development in the mountains. However, there is no reason to suspect either possibility in this instance since Lupine's stand is located in a remote section of western Oregon.

Important Concepts

Distribution of Income
Distribution Effects
Economic Rent
Economic Profit
Quasi-rent
Opportunity Cost
Specialization
Elasticity of Supply
Rate of Entry
Risk of Specialization
Monopoly Profit
Institutional Constraint
Expectations
Speed of Reaction
Education
Experience
Chance
Union Power
Natural Monopoly
Patent
Civil Service System
Complement
Substitute
Producer Surplus

12
Winners and Losers

Distribution Effects
of the Energy Crisis

A recurrent theme of the 1970s was the energy crisis, which reached its most visible point in the decade's last year. While specific events precipitated different manifestations, the underlying cause of the crisis remained clear: the world's petroleum supply is becoming increasingly tight. The central feature of the energy crisis is thus an accelerating increase in petroleum prices coupled with limited and/or uncertain availability. As consumers, almost all Americans suffer losses of varying magnitudes because of the energy crisis. However, as with all cataclysmic events, the distribution effects of the energy crisis will not fall evenly on the population. Rather, some Americans will benefit substantially from the energy crisis, while others will suffer losses beyond those incurred as consumers.

Indicate whether each of the individuals portrayed below will benefit or lose because of the energy crisis. What is the rationale for the gains or losses? What will be their magnitude? How long will they persist?

1. A recent petroleum engineering graduate living in Oklahoma. Four years of undergraduate education are required for the basic petroleum engineering degree.

2. The owner of a California corporation which is the first firm to manufacture and market a low-priced funnel which fits into the gas tank of late model cars designed to use unleaded gasoline. Employing this funnel a motorist can pump regular gas into his or her car—a procedure impossible otherwise because the nozzle on regular gas pumps is larger than the aperture of gas tanks on late model cars. One advantage of this procedure is that regular gasoline is lower priced than unleaded gasoline. More important, the former may be available when the latter is not.

177

3. An automobile salesperson working for an Illinois agency which sells primarily large American cars. She has been employed by this firm for two years.

4. The part owner of a medium-sized firm which has manufactured bicycles for twenty-five years. Located in North Carolina, the firm enjoys a comfortable niche in the bicycle market, albeit it is neither economically nor technologically dominant. This individual sits on the firm's board of directors, but is not employed by the corporation.

5. A Utah scientist with a doctorate in physics and additional advanced education in chemical engineering. Her specialty is the technology of oil shale extraction—a field in which she has worked for ten years.

6. A secretary employed by a solar energy firm in Arizona. He has worked for this small but expanding corporation for one year. The firm makes components for solar energy installations.

7. The owner of a northern Minnesota resort. Located on a beautiful lake, the resort features varied boating and other outdoor activities. In the past its clientele has been drawn not only from the Twin Cities, which are more than two hundred miles away, but also from states throughout the Middle West.

8. A Kentucky coal miner who belongs to the union. The union contract establishing the wages and fringe benefits to be paid to miners in this part of Kentucky will remain in force for two years.

9. An Ohio investor who one week ago purchased an unimproved parcel of land for eventual residential development. The tract of land is located in an outlying section of a metropolitan area, twenty-five miles from the center of the main city.

10. A Louisiana roustabout who has been employed by an oil-drilling firm for four years. A roustabout is a semiskilled worker who performs tasks of varied difficulty at the drilling site. No formal training is necessary for the position, but frequently roustabouts improve their skills through on-the-job experience.

11. A Connecticut businessman who undertakes free-lance assignments for corporations and others. His specialty is the Middle East where he has extensive experience and numerous contacts. His formal educa-

178

tion consists of an undergraduate degree, but he has become fluent in Arabic primarily through his work.

12. A middle-level manager in the Department of Energy, who lives in the Washington D.C. area. He has worked for the federal government for twenty years and was transferred to the Department of Energy two years ago. This individual is considered a good administrator who is highly familiar with government procedures. He is not recognized as having expertise specific to energy issues. Since beginning his government employment he has been covered by the "merit system" of federal employment administered by the Civil Service Commission. The essence of this system entails evaluation of a person by the commission as well as by the relevant government agency, and then placement of the person at an appropriate skill grade within the federal civil service.

13. The owner/manager of a small railroad in West Virginia. The track system is short but well-maintained. It is used exclusively to haul coal. The railroad is the only practical means of transporting coal from the mines that it serves. These mines are not owned by the railroad.

14. A Pennsylvania inventor who two years ago secured a patent on a new plastic which has several promising uses. The plastic is made primarily from petrochemicals. Like other patents in the United States, this patent gives the inventor, or his designees, the exclusive right to manufacture the new plastic for a period of seventeen years.

15. A California movie producer whose most recent film is about to be released. Initiated more than two years ago, it is an engaging and chilling story which centers on the hazards of heavy American dependence on foreign oil.

DISCUSSION

1. The increased price of petroleum will spur the search for new oil reserves and the development of petroleumlike substances such as shale oil and tar sands. Since petroleum engineers will be an important input in both activities, the demand for their services will increase. Because a specific degree is required to enter the profession, the supply of petroleum engineers will be somewhat inelastic. The increase in demand will therefore increase the wages of petroleum engineers. The Oklahoma petroleum engineering graduate will thus benefit because of the energy crisis.

This situation is illustrated in Figure 12-1. Initially the demand and supply curves are respectively D_0 and S_0. The energy crisis increases the demand for petroleum engineers to D_1. As a consequence, the wage rises from W_0 to W_1 and the quantity employed from Q_0 to Q_1.

Economic rent is defined as the payment to a productive resource in excess of its opportunity cost. The opportunity costs of different petroleum engineers are denoted by the supply curve. Only the Q_{1st} engineer is paid a wage equal to his opportunity cost. All other engineers are

Figure 12-1

Impact on Petroleum Engineers

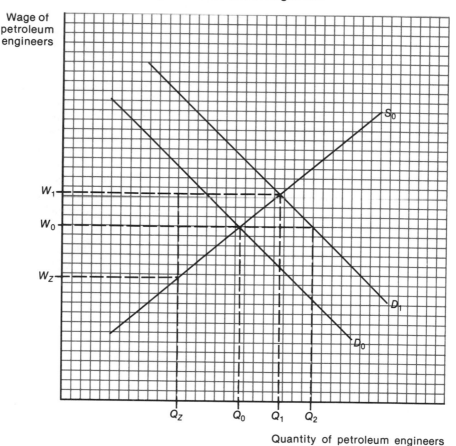

Quantity of petroleum engineers

paid their opportunity costs plus a rent. For example, the Q_{0th} engineer is paid his opportunity cost of W_0 and a rent equal to W_1 minus W_0.

From the standpoint of society economic rents present a varied picture. On the one hand, it is not necessary to pay the rent in order to keep the resource in the industry. The Q_{0th} engineer will continue to work as a petroleum engineer so long as he is not paid a wage lower than W_0, his opportunity cost. On the other hand, rents play the important role of allocating scarce resources among alternative uses at a given point in time. They also may call forth the production of additional resources, as will be discussed shortly.

As is true here, most wage increases are a combination of economic rents and opportunity cost payments. The rise in the wage from W_0 to W_1 draws Q_1 minus Q_0 engineers into the industry by paying their higher opportunity costs. It also increases the rents of the initial Q_0 engineers as well as paying smaller rents to the newly employed engineers. These increases in rents may seem inappropriate from a societal viewpoint, but this is not in fact true. Consider the results if the Q_1 minus Q_0 engineers are paid a wage of W_1 and the initial Q_0 engineers are paid a wage of W_0. Since their wage is W_0, the demand for the latter will equal Q_0 plus Q_2 minus Q_1. That is, an excess demand will exist for the Q_0 engineers. This excess demand will be eliminated when the wage is driven upward to W_1. The increase in rents thus serves the resource allocation function described above.

Economic rents constitute an unequivocal benefit to the individual. This benefit arises because the rent is the payment to the individual which exceeds the payment that he would receive in his next best opportunity. For example, in Figure 12–1 the Q_{Zth} engineer is paid his opportunity cost of W_Z and a rent equal to W_0 minus W_Z in the initial situation. The increase in demand produced by the energy crisis further increases his rent by the amount of W_1 minus W_0. The Q_{Zth} engineer therefore clearly benefits from the energy crisis.

Economic rents are similar to economic profits. In a fundamental sense they are identical since each constitutes payment beyond opportunity costs. They differ in terms of the mode of payment. Economic rent is paid to a productive resource in the form of wages or other payments, while economic profit is paid to the firm as a residual from its operations.

Like economic profits, economic rents serve the critical function of attracting new resources to an industry—a development that will occur in the petroleum engineer case. However, the rate of entry will be slowed by the educational requirements of the profession. Even so, these requirements are not overwhelming. The supply of petroleum engineers will thus increase significantly within several years, and the wage will decline as a result. The decrease in the wage will in turn diminish the economic rents earned by current petroleum engineers, including the recent graduate.

The Oklahoma engineer's gain from the energy crisis will thus be intermediate in duration. It will neither be eroded quickly nor will it persist for many years. The magnitude of his gain will also be intermediate. The reason is that while the new graduate is now a member of a skilled group, that group is reasonably large. Further, the recent graduate has not yet created for himself a position within his profession which would make him an even more specialized resource.

2. The energy crisis has spawned many interesting products, among them this unusual funnel. Its maker, the California corporation, will earn large economic profits but only for a short period of time. The uncertainty of unleaded gasoline availability will create a ready market for the funnel. Since the product is low priced, a high markup can be included in the price without appreciably diminishing the quantity demanded. Initial profit will thus be high.

However, the high level of profit will attract other firms to this market. Entry will be easy for almost any firm that produces metal products. It will thus be only a matter of months before other funnels are on the market. At that time competition will drive funnel prices rapidly downward, thereby substantially reducing and probably eliminating economic profits.

This case illustrates the importance of time. The owner of the California firm makes an economic profit because he moves quickly and is the first one to market the funnel. Conversely, his profits are short-lived because there are no factors slowing the entry of other firms. This case also illustrates the blurred distinction between economic profit and economic rent. Does this Californian benefit from the energy crisis by owning an innovative firm which makes an economic profit? Or, does he benefit by earning an economic rent on his entrepreneurial ability?

3. Since gasoline mileage of large American cars is usually at best modest, such cars and gasoline are complements. Because of this complementarity the sharp increase in gasoline prices will reduce the demand for large American cars. This result will have negative and perhaps disastrous consequences for the owners of the Illinois automobile agency. However, the salesperson will be largely insulated from these consequences. Despite the differences among cars, they are basically similar. Further, the critical element in sales is usually the ability to sell regardless of the specific product, as opposed to expertise in a particular area. A salesperson laid off by one automobile agency can thus usually find employment with another.

Therefore, if the Illinois salesperson finds her income falling or is laid off by her present employer, she will be able to move from her current firm to another firm (perhaps selling small cars) without undue difficulty. She may suffer to some extent because of temporary unemployment and/or the need to build up her stature at the new agency. Even so, her losses from the energy crisis will be modest and short-lived.

This case points up the importance of supply elasticity in determining distribution effects. If supply is completely elastic, the productive resource will not earn an economic rent. It will therefore not gain when demand rises. However, the converse is also true: The resource will not lose when demand falls. The supply of automobile salespeople, and of salespeople generally, is quite elastic. This supply elasticity limits the losses of the Illinois salesperson when the demand for large cars falls.

4. Bicycles and automobiles are substitutes, albeit imperfect ones. The higher price of gasoline increases the demand for bicycles by raising the costs of operating an automobile. Since the supply of bicycles is not completely elastic, the increase in demand will raise the price of bicycles. The North Carolina firm's profits will therefore increase at least in the short run. However, the firm is not dominant in the bicycle market from either an economic or technologic perspective. Its increased profits will therefore be eroded by the increased production of existing firms and by the entry of new firms.

The part owner of the firm will thus benefit from the energy crisis, but his gains will be intermediate in both magnitude and duration. These gains will be in the form of economic profits since he does not play an active management role in the corporation and thus does not earn a rent on his entrepreneurial or other abilities.

The California funnel maker earned economic profits because he reacted quickly to an opportunity. The Oklahoma petroleum engineer may have selected his field in part because he perceived the possibility of significant economic rents. No such foresight is evident here. This firm has manufactured bicycles for twenty-five years. It has been successful, but it is not an innovative force. It benefits from the energy crisis simply because it is in the right place at the right time. This illustrates the point that chance as well as ability plays an important role in the distribution of income.

Producer surplus is another concept used to analyze the distribution of income. It is the analogue in the product market of economic rent in the input market. It equals the difference between the price of the product and the opportunity costs of the firms producing the product.

This concept is illustrated in Figure 12–2 for the North Carolina bicycle firm. Assume for simplicity that this firm's bicycles carry a single marginal cost. The firm can therefore be represented in Figure 12–2 as the entity producing the Q_{Nth} quantity of bicycles. At initial equilibrium the firm is being paid its opportunity cost of P_N and a producer surplus of P_0 minus P_N. After the energy-related increase in bicycle demand the firm is still paid its opportunity cost of P_N, but now earns a higher producer surplus of P_1 minus P_N.

Producer surplus does not consist solely of economic profit. Rather, it is the sum of economic profits and economic rents earned by the resources used to produce the product. In some instances economic

Figure 12-2

Impact on Bicycles

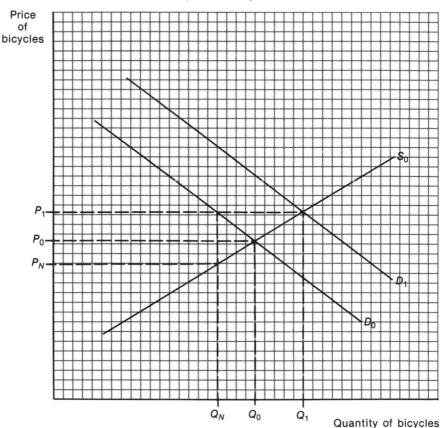

profits may predominate; in others economic rents. Further, as emphasized earlier, the distinction between the two is often hazy.

As suggested by their names, producer surplus is similar to consumer surplus, which was discussed in Chapter 5. The latter is the difference between the market price and the marginal valuation of the product by consumers. That is, consumer surplus equals the difference between the demand curve and the horizontal price line, while producer surplus equals the difference between the latter and the supply curve.

5. The increase in petroleum prices will stimulate the development of alternative energy sources, such as oil shale. The demand for people knowledgeable about oil shale extraction will thus increase. Further, demand will remain high for many years even if eventually after much effort oil shale extraction does not prove to be economically viable.

The Utah scientist is a highly specialized resource. The more specialized the resource, the more inelastic is the supply curve. The greater the inelasticity of supply, the larger will be the changes in economic rents produced by shifts in demand.

These points are illustrated in Figure 12–3. The initial demand and supply curves are D_0 and S_0, with the latter being highly inelastic, as is appropriate. S_H is a hypothetical supply curve which is much more elastic than S_0. Before the energy crisis the wage of oil shale experts is W_0 and the number employed is Q_0. With the advent of the crisis demand shifts outward to D_1. Since supply is highly inelastic, the results are a marked increase in the wage from W_0 to W_1 and a modest rise in the quantity employed from Q_0 to Q_1. However, if the more elastic S_H were the supply curve, the wage would rise only moderately to W_H, while the quantity employed would rise substantially to Q_H.

The Utah scientist is represented in Figure 12–3 as Q_U. Initially she is paid a wage of W_0, which consists of her opportunity cost of W_U and a rent equal to W_0 minus W_U. After the energy crisis she earns a wage of W_1 which is comprised of her opportunity cost of W_U and a rent equal to W_1 minus W_U. Her rent thus increases markedly because of the energy crisis. In fact, at the new equilibrium her rent is higher than her opportunity cost. However, if the more elastic supply curve, S_H, prevailed in this market, the Utah scientist would initially be paid her opportunity cost of W_E and a small rent equal to W_0 minus W_E. After the energy crisis her rent would rise to W_H minus W_E, but it would still be much smaller than her opportunity cost, W_E. Therefore, when demand increases, productive resources will capture much larger rents if their supply is inelastic rather than elastic.

Being a highly specialized resource, the Utah scientist will benefit strongly from the increased demand produced by the energy crisis.

Figure 12-3

Impact on Oil Shale Experts

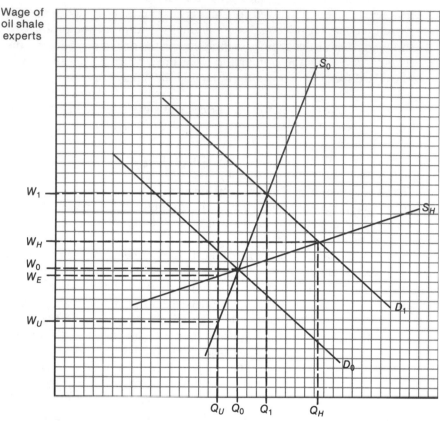

Quantity of oil shale experts

Further, she is well protected from the effects of entry. She has advanced education in two relevant disciplines and ten years of experience in the oil shale field. It will thus take much longer for other individuals to match her credentials than it will for new petroleum engineers to compete with the Oklahoma graduate.

6. Just as the energy crisis will spur the investigation of oil shale technology, so will it intensify the interest in solar energy. The demand for the Arizona firm's products will thus increase. However, this result will have little effect on the secretary. Many firms consider secretaries relatively interchangeable. A large pool of actual or potential secretaries exists in most areas. Because of both factors the supply of secretaries to most firms is highly elastic. That is, the secretarial wage is set by the prevailing conditions in the market and is independent of the particular circumstances of individual firms.

Since the energy crisis will not increase the overall demand for secretaries, their prevailing wage will not change appreciably. Because the Arizona secretary's wage is tied to the prevailing secretarial wage in the area, he will not benefit significantly from the energy crisis unless he has learned enough about the firm and/or solar energy that the firm's managers consider him superior to most other secretaries. In that event he may well earn an economic rent, but he does so by differentiating himself from other secretaries in the eyes of the firm's management.

This secretary is the converse of the Illinois automobile salesperson. The elasticity of supply cushions the latter against losses, while it prevents the former from securing major gains.

7. Although the owner may not have thought so until recently, this resort and gasoline are complements since the resort's customers must drive to northern Minnesota to use the resort. The higher price of gasoline will therefore reduce the demand for the resort's services. Less important, the resort uses petroleum products as an input in both its recreational and hotel services. The resort owner will thus be squeezed between decreasing demand and increasing cost.

His losses will be in several forms. As discussed in Chapter 6, a quasi-rent is the payment to a specialized durable resource in excess of its opportunity cost. In concept, quasi-rent is thus similar to economic rent or economic profit. In fact, the only difference between quasi-rent and economic rent is the nature of the resource earning the payment: Things earn quasi-rents and people earn rents.

The lodging and other facilities of the resort are major capital inputs. The quasi-rents on these inputs will decline, which may well be the major loss suffered by the owner. In addition, his economic profits and/or his economic rents on management and other abilities may decrease.

This case illustrates the reverse side of specialization. The resort owner cannot easily shift from northern Minnesota to Lake Minnetonka near Minneapolis. Similarly, even if she wanted to, the Utah scientist cannot readily switch from oil shale technology to urban sociology. In both instances the resources are highly specialized, and the decision to specialize was made before the energy crisis became highly visible. In the scientist's case specialization will yield great rewards; in the resort owner's case failure to take into account the energy crisis will produce losses.

The two cases together ilustrate the risk of specialization. Great gains can result from specialization, but so can total losses. The risk arises because the greatest benefits flow to those resources already specialized when an event or trend changes demand patterns. After-the-fact specialization is often unrewarding for two reasons. First, the new entrants, i.e., the after-the-fact specializers, will limit one another's gains. Second, since time is usually required to create a specialized resource, new events may transform demand patterns while the resource is being developed.

It is thus most advantageous to possess a specialized resource—whether labor, capital, or another input—before the market fully recognizes the value of the resource. However, such early possession entails the inherent risk that the demand for the resource will not develop to the extent expected. If this occurs, the result is likely to be a substantial loss since the specialized resource may have few alternative uses.

8. Since petroleum and coal are substitutes, the rise in the former's price will increase the demand for the latter. If there were no union, the Kentucky miner would share in the gains flowing from the increased demand to the extent that his mining skills are highly developed. The presence of the union changes the situation since it can influence the distribution of income. As discussed in Chapter 10, a union can increase the wage above the prevailing level even in a perfectly competitive labor market, albeit at the cost of reducing employment. In an oligopsonistic market, which at least certain coal-mining areas resemble, union pressure can increase both the wage and the number employed.

Eventually even if the Kentucky miner is relatively unspecialized, he will benefit from the energy crisis since the union will bargain away some of the mining firm's increased profits. However, he will not gain significantly until two years have passed because the existing contract will remain in effect for that period of time. Unionization is thus both a benefit and a cost to this miner. After two years his wages/fringe benefits and thus his economic rents will be higher than they would have been otherwise, but until that time the reverse will be true.

The more skilled the Kentucky miner, the less he will gain from unionization. If he is highly skilled, he may be able to bargain almost as high a wage as the union can and it would not be necessary to wait two years. However, if he is only semiskilled, his bargaining stance will be much weaker and he may not be able through his own efforts to increase his wage significantly either before or after two years.

The union contract is an example of an institutional constraint. Such a constraint imposes conditions on the market and thus alters the distribution of income. As is evident in this case, the distribution effects of the energy crisis are influenced by the term of the union contract.

That is, they would be different if the remaining term were not two years, but rather one or three years.

9. The increase in petroleum prices and the uncertainty about gasoline availability will decrease the value of this land. Hence, if this investor had purchased the land perhaps five years ago, she would suffer a loss due to the energy crisis. This loss would be in the form of a diminution in the land's economic rent.

However, the investor did not purchase the land five years ago but rather one week ago. At that time both she and the seller were aware of the energy crisis. The purchase price thus reflects the energy situation. Therefore, unless the investor or the seller made a serious error in estimating the effects of the energy crisis, the former will neither benefit nor lose significantly because of that crisis.

This case points up the importance of expectations in influencing the distribution of income. When the land changed hands, both the buyer and the seller knew about the energy crisis, and their expectations about that crisis are embodied in the purchase price. In a sense the energy crisis has been capitalized into the value of the land. In land, stock, and similar transactions, the critical element is not when the event occurs, but rather when expectations about the event develop.

Thus arises the curious paradox of the stock market modestly declining on good news. The reason is that the good news is already incorporated in the expectations of investors. That is, investors expect the event producing the good news to occur. Hence, when the event does occur, there is no rush of investors to buy, but rather the emergence of some sellers who wish to take their profits immediately.

10. Exploration for new oil reserves will be heightened by the increased price of petroleum since the rewards of finding oil are now greater. As a consequence, the demand for roustabouts will increase significantly. However, the supply of roustabouts is quite elastic since the position is semiskilled and no formal training is required. The higher demand for roustabouts will therefore increase the wage, and thus the economic rent, of roustabouts only to a modest extent.

The Louisiana roustabout resembles the Arizona secretary and the Illinois salesperson. In each case the supply of the personnel type is markedly elastic. Changes in demand therefore have little effect on the economic well-being of these three individuals. As with the Arizona secretary, the Louisiana roustabout will only benefit substantially from the energy crisis if he succeeds in substantially improving his skills through work experience. If he does so, he will earn an economic rent since his position can no longer be easily filled from the pool of semi-skilled labor.

11. The Connecticut businessman is similar to the Utah scientist. Both are highly specialized resources, and the demand for their types of resources will be increased substantially by the energy crisis. Both will thus earn much higher rents because of that crisis.

However, the Connecticut businessman and the Utah scientist differ in one important aspect—the source of the specialization. The special abilities of the Utah scientist are derived in part from her advanced education. Education does not play a similar role in contributing to the expertise of the businessman. This illustrates the general point that experience as well as education can create expertise and thus differentiate a resource from other resources. Further, as in this case, other individuals may find it as hard to match expertise derived from experience as expertise produced by a combination of education and experience. That being the case, the increased rents of the Connecticut businessman will persist for many years as will the higher rents of the Utah scientist.

12. The primary expertise of the federal employee is not in energy issues, but rather in administrative matters. His knowledge of government procedures enables him to smooth the flow of work within the federal system. Since this type of expertise is less valuable outside the federal government, the energy crisis will not encourage a private firm to strongly bid for this individual's services. The federal employee's economic rents will therefore not increase because of a shift to a higher-paying job in the private sector.

The civil service system of the federal government applies to the great majority of government workers, including this middle-level manager. It was designed to protect employees from political influence, but it also has the effect of insulating them from changes in demand. The energy crisis will increase government interest in energy issues, but this will not in turn increase wages and fringe benefits in the Energy Department. That is, although energy will be a hotter political issue than will commerce, employees at the same grade level and with the same tenure in the Energy and Commerce Departments will receive the same salary and benefits. This middle-level government manager will therefore not gain appreciably from the energy crisis.

The civil service system is another example of an institutional constraint. It secludes most government employees from market forces. As a result, changes in demand will not significantly influence their rents as long as they stay within the government. In this case the civil service system works to the disadvantage of the employee by preventing a moderate increase in economic rents. However, in other situations the system will protect employees from losses in rents due to declines in demand. The overall effect is to isolate the government from market signals. At times this is beneficial since it contributes to stability, but at other times it is deleterious because it makes the government more cumbersome and less responsive.

13. As noted earlier, coal and petroleum are substitutes. The rise in petroleum prices therefore increases the demand for coal which in turn leads to increases in the price and quantity produced of coal. Both of the latter results benefit this railroad. The increased coal production means that more coal will be shipped on this railroad. The higher price provides a margin which permits the railroad to raise its prices. The owner of this railroad will thus benefit substantially from the energy crisis.

This railroad is a monopoly. Part of its owner's gains will thus be in the form of higher monopoly profits. Such profits are a special type of economic profits. Like the latter, they are payments to the firm in excess of the opportunity costs of the resources used. They are singled out because they arise from the market position of the single seller. Usually the profits of oligopolists are also referred to as monopoly profits, although it would be more precise to term such profits oligopoly profits.

Like all railroads, this firm uses a large amount of capital equipment, which ranges from the rails themselves to coal cars. The higher demand for the railroad's services will increase not only its monopoly profits, but also the quasi-rents earned by these capital inputs. In addition, the owner of the railroad may earn economic rents on her managerial and other abilities.

This railroad is a natural monopoly. In this regard it resembles the toll road discussed in Chapter 8. Being a natural monopoly, the railroad is well protected from the incursions of possible competitors. Its gains from the energy crisis will therefore not only be large in magnitude, but also long in duration.

Because a natural monopoly has only distant competitors, it is rarely influenced significantly by their actions. However, a natural monopoly is highly sensitive to changes in demand, which can drastically alter the sum of economic profits, rents, and quasi-rents earned by the monopoly. This point is consonant with the emphasis throughout this chapter on specialization and the resulting inelasticity of supply. Since by definition a natural monopoly is the only producer in the relevant market, it is necessarily a unique and specialized firm.

191

14. The patent system is designed to encourage innovation. It does so by granting the inventor a patent which gives him or her the exclusive right to the new product or productive process for a period of seventeen years. That is, the patent confers on the inventor a monopoly right which is intended to reward his or her effort.

As suggested by their name, petrochemicals are derived from petroleum or natural gas. The increased prices of both commodities will drive petrochemical prices upward, which will in turn make it more expensive to produce the new plastic. The value of the monopoly right to the plastic conferred by the patent will thus be lower than it was before. The energy crisis will therefore reduce the monopoly profit of the Pennsylvania inventor, i.e., his return on the invention of the plastic.

15. Among the multitude of factors determining a film's popularity is the prevailing social, political, and economic climate of the day. A dominant factor in the current climate is the energy crisis. Since this film is woven around energy issues, its demand will be heightened by the energy crisis. The economic profits and/or rents of the California producer will therefore increase, perhaps dramatically.

Like many products, time is required to produce movies. During the production process, events can occur which drastically change the social, political, and economic climate. Such changes can be the dominant factor determining the profitability of the film since by the time the movie is completed it is a highly differentiated product which can only be changed at great cost.

Illustrating this point, suppose that the film in this case were addressed to an issue prominent throughout the early and middle 1970s: The efforts of an environmental quality director to reduce air pollution even at the cost of worsening gasoline mileage. Or, suppose that it were directed toward an issue of the 1960s: The endeavors of a poverty agency to improve the welfare of the urban poor. Unless there were marked differences in artistic quality, the popularity and thus the profitability of either suppositional film would be much lower than that of the film discussed above.

V

PUBLIC GOODS AND COLLECTIVE ACTION

This section addresses two related but different subjects. Both would have seemed largely foreign to the classical economists of the nineteenth century. Each is rooted in the twentieth century, where events have forced economists to consider these subjects. One subject is externalities and public goods. The other is government intervention in the marketplace, which is sometimes undertaken to remedy a public good or externality problem, but which also occurs for a wide variety of other reasons.

The model of perfect competition assumes that externalities are insignificant and that all important goods are private, which is to say that public goods are unimportant. These assumptions have become increasingly untenable in the modern world. Externalities and public goods are frequently present, and when present they pose difficult problems. These problems occur not only in large cities but also in small towns, as Chapter 13 makes clear. Its setting is Skylark, a hypothetical but realistic mountain resort in northern New England. Public goods and externalities abound in Skylark.

Mosquito control is a vexing issue in Fox Creek, a Skylark neighborhood. Crowding on the Skylark ski slopes is endemic during the high season. And even air pollution has become a feature of the Skylark scene.

The government itself has now become a major policy issue. No longer is it clear what the government should do or what it can do well. Chapter 14 takes up these issues by applying the central principle of benefit/cost analysis to five government programs. That is, it examines the probable net benefit of each program. Two of these programs are traditional government functions, i.e., utility regulation and provision of fire services. Another has a long history but is less frequently considered in economics—tax law provisions. Another is a relatively recent government activity, i.e., regulation of environmental quality. The remaining program is particularly controversial at this time: regulation of aircraft quality by the Federal Aviation Administration.

Important Concepts

Public Good
Externality
External Cost
External Benefit
Free-rider Phenomenon
Collective Action
Private Good Inducement
Negotiation
Strategic Bargaining
Independence Within Large Group
Interdependence Within Small Group
Peak Load Pricing
Price Discrimination
Crowding Costs
Excess Demand
Common Property
Exclusion Principle
Joint Consumption
Differentiated Oligopoly
Perfect Competition
Vertical Summation of Demand
Horizontal Summation of Demand

13
Problems in Paradise

A Galaxy of Public Goods and Externalities

Skylark is a famous mountain resort in northern New England. While hypothetical, it resembles other resorts in the Northeast and elsewhere in the country. Most of its visitors are from the Northeast and adjacent Canada, but its renown is such that it attracts people from throughout the United States as well as from foreign countries. While Skylark's population is hard to pinpoint since it fluctuates dramatically during the year, about four thousand people count themselves as permanent residents. The area's permanent population is steadily expanding as people move to Skylark attracted by its ambiance and recreational opportunities.

Skylark has three seasons of high activity; each has its characteristic flavor. In summer the emphasis is upon a variety of outdoor recreation, ranging from bicycling on special trails to boating on neighboring lakes. In autumn the highpoint is the brilliantly hued foliage cloaking the nearby mountains. In winter the primary focus is alpine skiing, although cross-country skiing and ice-skating are also popular. In all seasons Skylark's atmosphere is cosmopolitan, reflecting both the quality of its services and the diversity of its guests and residents. The town offers a broad range of accomodations, restaurants, and entertainments.

1. Fox Creek is a Skylark neighborhood several miles from the core area. It is situated in a mountain valley along the creek of the same name. Ninety households reside in Fox Creek, either in houses or duplexes. The area has no condominiums. The quality of construction in Fox Creek is generally high, although the dwellings in the area are not uniform, differing in style, size, and other characteristics.

During the summer mosquitoes are a persistent nuisance in Fox Creek. Each household spends about $30 per year on personal antimosquito measures, such as repellents and outdoor smudge pots. None of these measures is particularly effective, and each household continues to be bothered by the mosquito nuisance. If Fox Creek were carefully sprayed three times a year with non-DDT insecticides, the mosquito population would be drastically reduced. As a result, even if all personal antimosquito measures were abandoned, each household would be less bothered by mosquitoes than it is now. The cost of spraying Fox Creek would be $300 per application, or $900 per year.

Is mosquito control in Fox Creek a public good?

2. None of the Fox Creek households undertakes on its own initiative to spray the community in the manner described above. Why not?

3. Three Fox Creek households have boggy areas on their land, which serve as excellent breeding places for mosquitoes. These households are situated on different small tributaries of Fox Creek at some distance from each other. It has been estimated that simple drainage work undertaken once a year would substantially reduce the mosquito-breeding capacity of the boggy areas. The cost for each of these households would be $150 per year.

Even if community-wide spraying were not performed, the drainage of these boggy areas would significantly diminish the mosquito nuisance. The two steps together would essentially eliminate the mosquito problem in Fox Creek. These three households dislike mosquitoes as much as the other Fox Creek households. Yet none of the former has drained the boggy area on its property. Why not?

4. While discussing the mosquito problem, Martha Exner and several other Fox Creek residents note that community-wide spraying and drainage of the boggy areas would be much more effective in reducing the mosquito nuisance than are the personal measures now practiced by Fox Creek households. They also observe that the annual cost of spraying and draining would be $1,350, which is half the current combined expenditures of Fox Creek households on antimosquito measures. It therefore seems clear that Fox Creek households would be better off if they carried out the spraying and drainage efforts than they are at present.

Martha's group concludes that the best approach would be to establish an informal organization which would solicit voluntary contributions from Fox Creek households to pay for spraying and drainage. These Fox Creek residents also decide that it would be prudent to allow an annual cushion of $270, which could be used to cover both unexpected costs as well as minor administrative expenses. The addition of this cushion brings total annual costs to $1,620, or $18 per Fox Creek household. Led by Martha, the informal organization will therefore ask each of the ninety Fox Creek households to contribute $18 per year for spraying and drainage.

Is this voluntary effort likely to succeed in controlling the mosquito nuisance?

5. Is the voluntary effort likely to be more successful in each of the following circumstances?

a. The requested contribution is increased to $25, but an imaginative and well-planned party is included as a benefit. Only those contributing may attend the party.

b. The number of households involved is fifteen, rather than ninety, and the spraying/drainage costs are reduced proportionately.

6. The voluntary effort is conducted as described in Question 4. It does not succeed in raising sufficient dollars to pay the costs of community-wide spraying and drainage of the boggy areas. Discussing its failure with several Fox Creek friends, Don Sherwood recalls that there is a Fox Creek Property Owners' Association. At present the association's main activity is to review building plans in order to assure that new construction will adhere to the standards specified in the Fox Creek covenants. However, this association has the power to levy assessments for certain purposes on Fox Creek households. If less than $500 per household, an assessment must be approved by two-thirds of the households attending a meeting for this purpose, provided that a quorum of at least one-third of the households is present at the meeting. If $500 or more per household, an assessment must be approved, either in person or by proxy, by two-thirds of all Fox Creek households. While this assessment power is limited to specific purposes, one of these is insect control.

Several days later Don meets with the officers of the Fox Creek Property Owners' Association. The latter concur that mosquito control would enhance the quality of life in the Fox Creek area and that such control can be attained by assessing each household $18 per year. A meeting is called to which all Fox Creek households are invited; its purpose is to review and approve or disapprove a resolution prepared by Don. This resolution would assess each Fox Creek household $18 per year, with the proceeds to be used to drain the boggy areas and to conduct community-wide spraying.

Assuming that a quorum of Fox Creek households attends the meeting, will Don's resolution be approved?

7. The Globe Theater in Skylark is justly famed for the quality of its dramatic presentations given each summer. Are these presentations a public good?

8. Excellent restaurants abound in Skylark; they offer a range of cuisines to visitors and residents. No formal connection exists between any Skylark restaurant and the Globe Theater. Does the Globe affect Skylark restaurants? Do the restaurants affect the Globe?

9. The Skylark ski area is operated by the Skylark Corporation, which charges the same ticket prices throughout the ski season. While capacity is large, Skylark attracts many skiers. It is thus unusual if there is not at least a short line at most lifts. Crowding is especially severe during high season which includes Christmas vacation, weekends in February and March, and spring/Easter vacation. At these times long lift lines are commonplace and congestion on the ski slopes is a problem, sometimes a severe one. The town's facilities are also overtaxed during high season. Parking lots are overflowing; an empty hotel or condominium room is a rarity; and restaurant reservations may be almost unattainable unless secured several days in advance.

Faced with this situation, the Skylark Corporation adopts a new pricing policy. Under this policy ticket prices will be raised by 25 percent during the high season; they will remain unchanged during the remainder of the ski year.

Will this new policy increase the profits of the Skylark Corporation? Will most people who ski at Skylark support this change?

10. Air pollution is often considered to be primarily a problem of large metropolitan areas, but this is not always true. Skylark, a mountain resort, has such a problem, with the main pollution sources being automobiles and fireplaces. The great majority of Skylark residents and visitors would prefer to reduce air pollution in the area. Yet they continue to drive cars and use fireplaces much as they always have. What factors underlie this seeming contradiction?

11. Lake Allen and Lake Webster are two lakes of similar size near Skylark. The former is publicly owned in the sense that it is administered by the state government. On its eastern shore is a small state park which has boat-launching facilities. The state does not routinely patrol or otherwise actively manage Lake Allen. Only a state fishing license is required to fish in the lake.

In contrast, Lake Webster is privately owned. Its owner maintains a park with launching facilities on its western shore. A state license is also required to fish in this lake, but in addition the owner charges daily fees equal to $10 per boat and $10 per fisherman. Poaching is difficult on this lake since the only practical point of entry is through the owner's facility.

The two lakes are equally accessible to Skylark. Fishing intensity was low on both lakes a decade ago, at which time the quality of fishing in the two lakes was judged to be similar. Since that time fishing interest throughout the Skylark area has increased markedly. Neither the private owner nor the state government have stocked the respective lakes with small fish. Neither lake attracts sailboats, water-skiers, or large power boats.

At present which lake is likely to have more fishermen on a given day? On which lake is there a greater likelihood of catching more and/or larger fish?

DISCUSSION

1. To be a public good, an item must meet two conditions. First, joint consumption must be possible. That is, one person's consumption of the good must not significantly interfere with another's consumption. Second, the exclusion principle must not apply. That is, if the good is provided for one person, it must be very difficult to exclude others from consuming it.

Mosquito control in Fox Creek meets both of these criteria. One household's enjoyment of mosquito scarcity will not hinder another's consumption of the same good. If mosquito density is sharply reduced in Fox Creek, all families in the area will benefit. Mosquito control in the neighborhood is therefore a public good.

Because of the joint consumption and nonexclusion properties, the market demand for a public good equals the vertical summation of individuals' demand curves. Since all Fox Creek households must consume the same quantity of mosquito control, the different prices which different households are willing to pay for a certain quantity of mosquito control are added together to determine what the entire community will pay for that quantity of mosquito control. This process is repeated for other quantities of mosquito control in order to determine Fox Creek's demand for this good.

This process is illustrated in Figure 13-1 for two Fox Creek households, Y and Z, whose respective demand curves for mosquito control are P_Y and P_Z. For Q_0 amount of mosquito control, Household Y will pay P_Y and Household Z, P_Z. Since the two households must perforce consume mosquito control together, the total price which they will pay for Q_0 mosquito control is P_M, which equals the sum of P_Y and P_Z.

In contrast, the market demand for a private good, such as the bread of the Black Diamond Bakery in Chapter 6, is calculated by horizontally summing individuals' demand curves. This procedure is depicted in

Figure 13-1

Determination of Market Demand for Mosquito Control

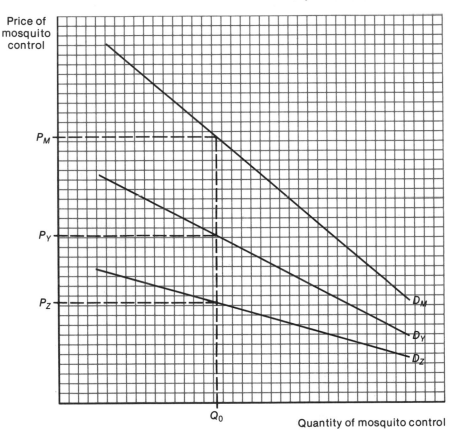

Figure 13-2

Determination of Market Demand for Bread

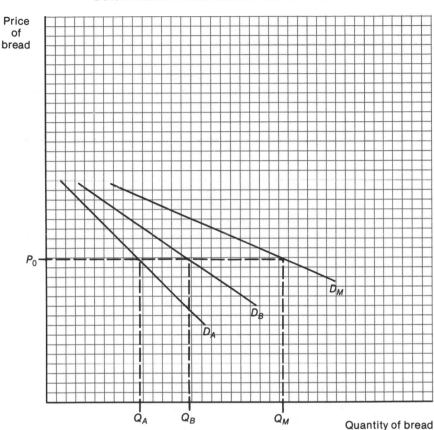

Figure 13−2. At price P_0, Individual A will purchase Q_A bread, and Individual B, Q_B bread. The quantity of bread demanded by this market of two individuals at price P_0 is therefore Q_M, which equals Q_A plus Q_B.

2. The ninety Fox Creek households together are willing to spend at least $2,700 for better mosquito control, since they are now spending that amount for personal antimosquito measures. However, no single household places a value as high as $870 on mosquito reduction. That sum would be the net cost to a household if it undertook the spraying procedure, i.e., the gross spraying cost of $900 minus the $30 that would be saved because personal antimosquito measures would no longer be necessary. Since the benefit derived from spraying would be less than the net cost, no single household will unilaterally spray the Fox Creek area.

3. If one of these households drains the boggy areas on its property, it would pay the entire cost, but would reap only part of the benefit. While the reduction in mosquito density would probably be greatest for the household and its neighbors, the benefit derived by the household would still not be sufficient to justify the cost of drainage. None of the three households is thus willing to drain the boggy areas.

This case illustrates the importance of externalities. The presence of the boggy areas imposes costs on Fox Creek households, but only a small fraction of these costs are experienced by the decision maker—the property owner in this case. Most of the costs are external to the decision maker, and are thus termed external costs. The property owner does not take into account these external costs in deciding whether to drain the boggy areas. He therefore does not undertake such drainage.

Similarly, the drainage work can be regarded as an activity with important external effects. Viewed from this perspective, the property owner bears the entire cost, but secures only a small portion of the benefit. That is, the drainage of the boggy areas produces significant external benefits for other Fox Creek households. However, the property owner does not consider these external benefits in reaching a drainage decision, and he thus does not drain the boggy areas.

4. The ninety households in Fox Creek constitute a large group, albeit not a huge one. The larger the group, the less interdependence among its members. This factor will be somewhat offset in Fox Creek because many households know each other. Even so, any single household can legitimately conclude that the success of the voluntary effort is independent of its actions. That is, the effort is as likely to succeed if the household does not contribute as if the household contributes. That being the case, why contribute?

This characteristic of large groups pursuing public goods is termed the free-rider phenomenon. Since one member's actions do not materially influence whether the group provides the public good, each group member is tempted to take a free ride on the provision of the public good by other group members. To better understand the forces creating the free-rider phenomenon, consider the Fox Creek case further. If the voluntary effort succeeds, a representative family will enjoy the scarcity of mosquitoes whether or not it contributes to the effort. In fact, it will be better off if it does not contribute since it will then save the $18. Conversely, if the voluntary effort fails, the representative family will be in a better position if it does not contribute, because even if the money is returned, it is likely to be a matter of weeks before this occurs.

Since each member of a large group has an incentive to act as a free rider, many will do so. When that occurs, the group will not be able to provide the public good. The free-rider phenomenon thus subverts the ability of large groups to provide public goods for their members. Therefore, unless social cohesion among the Fox Creek households is extremely strong, the voluntary effort to control mosquitoes will not succeed. Some households will contribute, but many will not, citing a variety of reasons for their failure to do so. As a result, the voluntary effort will not raise sufficient funds to cover the costs of spraying and drainage.

5a. While the size of the contribution is now larger, the donor receives a private good as well as a public good. A household can still conclude that it is not in its interests to contribute, but it cannot hope to free ride and still go to the party. Some households will thus be induced to abandon the free-rider stance. The voluntary effort is therefore more likely to succeed now than it was before.

This case illustrates how a large group may succeed in providing a public good for its members if it packages that good with the private good. The rationale is that the private good inducement overrides at least to some extent the free-rider phenomenon. Many industry associations operate in this manner. Examples range from the American Farm Bureau Federation to state nursing home associations. The organizations succeed at least in part because they offer combinations of public and private goods to their members.

5b. Reducing the size of the group will drastically alter the interaction among its members. If only fifteen households are involved, a household can no longer assume that its actions will not influence the actions of the group. Each household's contribution will now be 1/15, rather than 1/90, of the total. More important, one household's decision to contribute will influence the decisions of others. Further, in a small group all members will be aware of one another's actions. Strong social pressure can thus be exerted on recalcitrant members.

A small group is thus more likely to be successful in providing a public good than is a large group. This is true even if a small group member elects to strategically bargain by refusing to pay after most members have committed themselves. The reason for the small group's success is that the free-rider phenomenon is not viable in a small group. It is based on the presumption that one member's actions do not influence what the group does. This presumption is justified in a large group, but it is untenable in a small group. It is thus the interdependence within the small group which overcomes the free-rider phenomenon and increases the likelihood that the group will be able to provide the public good.

Because of the interdependence among small group members, negotiation and strategic bargaining are prominent features of their interaction. These two processes are similar in conduct, but different in purpose. Both entail discussions as well as at times written communications among group members. The aim of negotiation is to protect one's interests, but still to reach an agreement with other group members. Strategic bargaining downplays the agreement aspect and concentrates on the procurement of a large gain, usually at the group's expense. An excellent opportunity for strategic bargaining occurs if a unanimous vote is required for an action and if all but one member have voted affirmatively.

Negotiation and strategic bargaining are pointless in a large group since one member's actions do not influence what the group does as a whole. Similarly, in a large group the actions of any two members do not appreciably affect each other's situation. That being the case, why negotiate or bargain?

Differentiated oligopoly and perfect competition are excellent examples of small and large groups respectively. As emphasized in Chapter 9, interdependence is a distinctive feature of differentiated oligopoly. The producers in this market structure are well aware that the actions of one affect the positions of others. In perfect competition the converse is true. As a consequence, no producer has any concern about the actions taken by any other single producer.

In any industry, a public good enjoyed by all producers is higher prices for their products. Being a small group, oligopolists can establish a collusive agreement designed to raise prices, albeit only after substantial negotiation. However, since perfect competitors constitute a large group, it is exceedingly difficult for them to increase prices through collusion, because each producer is tempted to act as a free rider.

6. At present each Fox Creek household is paying $30 per year for antimosquito measures. If Don's resolution passes, each household will pay $18 per year and the mosquito nuisance will be much smaller. The resolution will therefore be approved by the great majority of those attending the meeting.

As illustrated here, collective action is another way to overcome the free-rider phenomenon. In this instance a household is not considering whether to pay $18 for mosquito control, uncertain as to what other households will do. Rather, the household is deciding whether it and all other households should pay $18 each for mosquito control. Since the assessment will be imposed on all households, no opportunity exists for any household to act as a free rider.

7. The Globe's offerings are not public goods. It is true that they meet one of the conditions for a public good. They can be jointly consumed. That is, ignoring noisy coughers and their ilk, one person's enjoyment of the play does not usually interfere with another's consumption of the same good. However, the other public good criterion does not hold for Globe presentations. It is not true that if the good is provided for one, it must be provided for all. It is entirely possible to furnish the good to some individuals and to exclude others. All that is necessary is to sell tickets; those with tickets are admitted and those without tickets are not.

Many goods are similar to Globe presentations in that they may be jointly consumed, but the exclusion principle applies. Examples are Skikamagua theater showings in Chapter 9 and Magic Carpet travel in Chapter 8. The joint consumption property of these goods differentiates them from products, such as oranges or haircuts, which cannot be jointly consumed. However, the exclusion property differentiates them even more strongly from public goods. Unlike the latter, it will not be necessary to resort to collective action, small group negotiation, or private good inducements to attain a sufficient supply of joint consumption goods like Globe presentations.

8. The Globe Theater attracts visitors to Skylark, which increases the demand for restaurant services. The restaurants enhance Skylark's reputation as a resort, which increases the demand for the Globe's presentations. While there is no formal tie between the Globe Theater and Skylark restaurants, their operations are synergistic. Each exerts a favorable influence on the other. That is, each confers external benefits on the other.

This case points up that externalities need not be negative. At times they are, as illustrated by the Fox Creek boggy areas. However, often they are not. Stores in a shopping center may benefit one another as may physicians or lawyers in the same office building. At the consumption level the pride that a homeowner takes in his beautiful lawn may be greatly appreciated by his neighbors.

9. The high season exhibits the classic characteristics of excess demand. At this time demand exceeds supply and crowding results. In this situation the ticket price increase will have two beneficial effects for the Skylark Corporation. First, high-season profits will increase since the quantity of tickets sold will not decline by 25 percent. Second, low-season profits may also rise as some skiers react to the price change by shifting from the high season to other times of the ski year. The new policy will therefore increase the profits of the Skylark Corporation.

During the high season skiers impose substantial crowding costs on each other. At this time skiers thus pay two prices—one the ticket price and the other in the form of crowding costs. The new policy will increase the ticket price, but it will reduce the crowding costs. Skier support of the policy depends upon the extent to which the latter occurs. As noted above, the price change will not reduce skier volume by 25 percent. However, a 10 percent decrease in skier volume on congested days may be sufficient to markedly diminish crowding costs. If the new policy does succeed in significantly reducing crowding costs, it is likely that most skiers will support the pricing change.

The term applied to the pricing change discussed here depends upon the perspective. From a profit-maximizing viewpoint the new policy is a form of price discrimination. It is beneficial to the firm since profits can be increased by charging a higher price during the high season and a lower price during the rest of the ski year. From a welfare-maximizing standpoint the new policy is an example of peak load pricing. It is also advantageous from this standpoint since crowding costs are a real cost to society. Therefore, to maximize society's welfare, a higher price should be charged during the peak demand period in order to reduce crowding costs. In the context of Chapter 8 if Grundleschlotchen or Fairenweather were operating the ski area, either would charge a higher price during the high season, albeit not necessarily the same price.

Peak load problems are common since consumers frequently impose crowding costs on one another. Examples include airplanes stacked over airports on Friday afternoons, electricity use on hot summer days, and golfers lined up to play at neighborhood courses on weekends. In each case the root of the problem is that the use of a resource during a specific time period is undervalued. The remedy is straightforward: The price for using the resource during the peak demand period should be increased. In most instances either profit maximization or welfare maximization will provide this remedy, although the magnitude of the price differential may differ. The difficulty arises when a resource is managed with an eye to neither welfare maximization nor profit maximization. In such situations the peak load problem may become severe as users impose large crowding costs on one another.

10. Air pollution is a classic case of externalities. The use of the car or fireplace conveys important benefits and significant losses. Almost all of the former flow to the individuals involved, while they experience only a small fraction of the latter. Therefore, from the individual's perspective the benefits of automobile or fireplace use outweigh the costs, since most of the costs are external to the individual. That being the case, each individual continues to use the car or fireplace in his or her customary manner, and air pollution remains a problem in Skylark.

Air pollution can also be analyzed from a public-good perspective. Improved air quality is the public good sought by Skylark residents and visitors. Such individuals are numerous and constitute a large group. Each individual in the group thus has an incentive to act as a free rider by continuing to use his car or fireplace in an unrestricted manner. This position is rational from the free rider's standpoint since the emissions from his car or fireplace will not materially influence air pollution in the town. Since all Skylark residents and visitors are tempted to act as free riders, many do so, and air pollution continues to be a problem.

11. Since the price for fishing is much higher on Lake Webster than on Lake Allen, the number of fishermen will be greater on the latter. However, unless fishing intensity is low, the greater the number of fishermen, the fewer and smaller will be the fish. The likelihood of catching more and/or larger fish is therefore greater on Lake Webster.

Strictly speaking, Lake Allen is not owned in common, but is managed like a common property resource. That is, although use of the lake is valuable, no charge is made for this use. The zero price undervalues the resource and leads to overuse.

The result of common property management in Lake Allen's case is that too many fishermen fish in the lake. The eventual consequence is a diminution in the quality of fishing. If overfishing is sufficiently severe, the lake may not replenish itself especially since it is not being periodically stocked. If this occurs, fishing quality may become so low that even with the large price differential there will now be more fishermen on Lake Webster than on Lake Allen. This illustrates the point that overuse of the resource through common property management can lead to irreparable damage, whether the resource be fish in a lake or fresh water in an underground pool damaged by salt water intrusion.

Pointing up the interrelationships among public goods, externalities, and common property, air pollution in Skylark can also be analyzed as a common property problem. Under this approach the resource owned in common is the air. Zero price is placed on using the air as a waste receptacle. As a consequence, too many emissions are released from automobiles and fireplaces, with the result that air pollution becomes a problem in Skylark.

209

Important Concepts

Government Intervention
Benefit/Cost Analysis
Net Benefit
Public Interest
Bureau Interests
Distribution Effects
Welfare Maximization
Economic Efficiency
Marginal Social Gain
Marginal Social Cost
Welfare Loss
Government Regulation
Monopoly
Public Good
Externality
Capture of Regulatory Agency
Taxes as Regulatory Mechanism
Effluent Fee
Quality Regulation
Consumer Knowledgeability
Information Costs
Enforcement Costs

14

The Public Sector at Work

Benefits and Costs of Government Intervention

A dominant development of the twentieth century has been the growth of government. In 1900 government in this country maintained a low profile, the general feeling being that the less government the better. Since then government especially at the federal level has gradually assumed an increasing number of responsibilities. As a result, government is now a highly complex institution whose influence on American society is pervasive.

Two decades ago it was widely acknowledged in this country that government enlargement would continue—a conclusion welcomed by liberals but begrudgingly admitted by conservatives as well. Now the atmosphere has changed. No longer is government expansion considered inevitable or desirable. Not just conservatives but a broad range of people question the effectiveness of government. The proper role of government in American society has become uncertain.

It is thus particularly appropriate at this time to examine different government roles. An excellent tool for this purpose is benefit/cost analysis. In its more refined forms, this type of analysis strives to quantify with at least some precision all benefits and costs. Such quantification is beyond the scope of this book, but the central principle of benefit/cost analysis is not. It is to identify the major benefits and costs of an ongoing or planned activity, and to thus determine the net benefit of the acitvity.

Five government programs are described below. Assess the benefits and costs of each program from a public interest perspective, i.e., from the standpoint of improving society's welfare, at a minimum the announced objective of government. As an important step in this process, search in each case for the rationale underlying the program. Based in part upon this rationale, is it likely that the program's benefits substantially exceed its costs, so that the program's net benefit is significantly positive? Or, is it uncertain without more detailed analysis which is larger—the benefits or the costs? Or, is it probable that the program's net benefit is negative, i.e., that the program's benefits are distinctly lower than its cost? If the latter, does the program have distributional effects which may explain at least in part its continued existence?

In evaluating the following programs do not assume that government workers (i.e., bureaucrats) have perfect knowledge. Similarly, do not assume that they maximize the public interest. At times they may, but analysis increasingly suggests that more often they maximize bureau interests, i.e., the size and power of their agency. Also do not presume that producers and consumers will not attempt to influence regulatory agencies. Rather, drawing on the principles of group interaction discussed in the previous chapter, operate on the presumption that both producers and consumers would like to influence government regulators, but that the former will usually be more successful in this regard since they often constitute a small group, whereas the latter comprise a large group. In short, proceed on the justifiable basis that interest groups will strive to influence government agencies and that such agencies will maximize an amalgam of bureau interests and the public interest.

1. Electric utilities are regulated by state government, often by an independent board sometimes termed the public utilities commission. The function of these utilities is to provide electricity to industrial, residential, and other users. While there may be several utilities in a state, all areas within the state are allocated to one or another utility. A customer is thus not able to choose among utilities. In all states there are far more customers than utilities. The precise duties of public utilities commissions vary to some extent among states, but in all instances their main task is to review and approve the rates charged by the utility.

2. A traditional responsibility of local government in this country is protection against fire. Fire districts may be composed of an entire city or a sparsely populated rural area. Fire departments may be staffed by professional fire fighters who are municipal employees, or by local volunteers who serve only when the need arises. In some areas fire protection services may be provided by commercial firms under contract to local government. Most fire departments offer preventive services, but their main function remains therapeutic, i.e., to extinguish fires once they have started.

3. The *Internal Revenue Code* is a monument of complexity. Among its provisions is the stipulation that individuals may deduct all interest payments from their federal income taxes. Interest on home mortgages comprises the largest fraction of these deductions, with interest on car loans, other installment loans, and credit card purchases also contributing significantly to the total.

4. A role only recently assumed by government is preservation and enhancement of environmental quality. A central objective in this field is improvement in water quality, or conversely, reduction in water pollution. At the federal level the Environmental Protection Agency has the lead responsibility. At state and local levels a diversity of governments are involved, ranging from municipalities to regional consortiums. To effect improvements in water quality, pollution control agencies can potentially employ a range of techniques. The latter include publicizing instances of severe pollution, constraining the actions of polluters through regulations, and placing effluent fees on the discharge of pollutants.

5. The recent difficulties experienced by DC-10s have spotlighted a major function of the Federal Aviation Administration (FAA). This function is to develop and enforce standards for the manufacture, operation, and maintenance of commercial aircraft. Only a few firms manufacture such aircraft; all are large corporations. The main purchasers of commercial aircraft are the commercial airlines, which are also large organizations. Like the aircraft manufacturers, the airlines employ a diversity of people, many of whom have extensive education and / or experience in technical areas.

DISCUSSION

1. Like the toll road in Chapter 8 and the railroad in Chapter 12, the electric utility is a natural monopoly. From a public interest perspective the problem with a monopoly is that a profit-maximizing monopolist produces too little product. This point is illustrated in Figure 14–1. Like Grundleschlotchen in Chapter 8, a profit-maximizing utility equates marginal revenue with marginal cost. It therefore produces Q_0 electricity and charges a price of P_0.

A welfare-maximizing utility, like Fairenweather in Chapter 8, operates at the point where the marginal gain to society equals the marginal

Figure 14-1

Welfare Loss Due to Monopoly

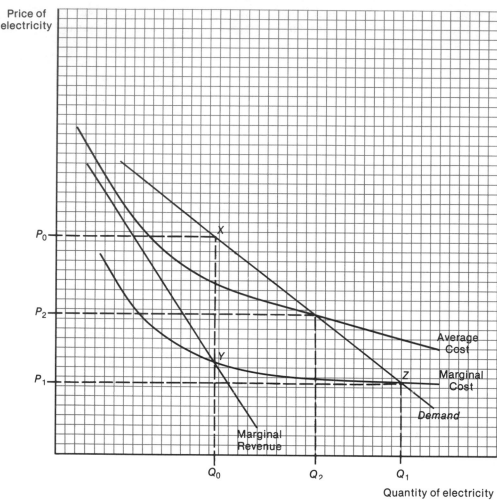

cost to society. That is, it equates marginal social gain with marginal social cost. Presuming that the demand and cost curves do not incorporate significant externalities, marginal social cost equals the utility's marginal cost and marginal social gain equals the price consumers are willing to pay, as denoted by the utility's demand curve. The welfare-maximizing utility therefore operates at the point where the marginal cost curve intersects the demand curve. It thus charges a price of P_1 and produces an output of Q_1.

Economic efficiency is attained in an industry when marginal social gain equals marginal social cost. The objective of welfare maximization is therefore to achieve economic efficiency. If marginal social gain and marginal social cost are not equal, economic efficiency is not attained and the result is a welfare loss. This occurs in the monopoly case under profit maximization. At output Q_0 marginal social gain exceeds marginal social cost, and continues to do so until output Q_1 is reached. The welfare loss incurred by having Q_0 rather than Q_1 electricity is the benefit of the additional electricity minus the cost of producing it, i.e., the difference between the demand and marginal cost curves between Q_0 and Q_1. The welfare loss thus equals the approximately triangular figure XYZ.

From a public interest perspective the objective of regulation is to reduce the welfare loss by forcing the utility to produce an output closer to Q_1. As discussed in Chapter 8, one difficulty with marginal cost pricing in a natural monopoly is that price will be lower than average cost, thereby necessitating a politically unpopular government subsidy. Another problem with marginal cost pricing is that it may be difficult to determine the utility's marginal cost. At a minimum it will be easier to estimate average cost than marginal cost. These two considerations have led many utility commissions to employ average cost pricing, i.e., to force the utility to charge a price of P_2 and to produce an output of Q_2. However, as also noted earlier, average cost pricing changes the utility's incentives and may induce an upward creep in the firm's cost curves.

Utility regulation may thus flounder because marginal cost pricing may not be feasible and because average cost pricing may not be very satisfactory. Equally important, utility regulation presents a classic opportunity for producers to "capture" the regulatory agency. There are only a few utilities in each state, whereas there are many consumers, ranging from large industrial plants to small households. The utility commission's decisions will have a major impact on utility firms; they will appreciably influence consumers but to a much lesser extent. The utility firms thus have strong reasons for influencing the commission, and being a small group, they are likely to be able to do so. In contrast, individual consumers will be less inclined to expend energy influencing the commission since each has less at stake. Further, since they comprise a large group, they will encounter the usual problems that such groups have in organizing effective actions.

Capture of a regulatory agency by the industry infrequently occurs through direct bribes or other illegal actions. Rather, it arises in a more subtle and gradual way. The utility firms maintain good contacts with the commission; they present well-documented cases; they employ experts to shore up certain points; and they respond promptly to the commission's requests. The result is that the commission frequently hears the industry's point of view presented in a persuasive manner. It is thus drawn almost imperceptibly to that viewpoint.

Capture of a regulatory agency does not necessarily ruin its effectiveness. Often, as with electric utilities, expertise is required to effectively regulate. Uninformed regulation can grossly distort an industry and may be worse than no regulation at all. Even so, capture of a regulatory agency is likely at a minimum to soften the tone of the agency's decisions. That is, the agency's stance will not be stridently antiproducer. Or using a more concrete example, presuming that the commission is employing average cost pricing, it might be inclined to let the average cost curve slip upward, with the result that the utility's output would no longer be Q_2 in Figure 14–1, but rather a quantity somewhat lower than Q_2, albeit higher than Q_0.

On balance, marginal cost pricing in utility regulation is attractive in theory, but difficult in practice. Average cost pricing is usually feasible, but introduces unfavorable incentives. At least partial capture of the utility commission is common because of the nature of this regulatory environment. However, the costs of operating utility commissions are low compared to the potential gains through regulation. In addition, enforcement costs are almost nonexistent since utility rates are widely disseminated.

It is therefore likely that the benefits of utility regulation exceed its costs, but that the difference is not as great as many imagine. Referring back to Figure 14–1, government intervention probably leads to an output higher than Q_0, but not that much higher. Even so, the gains from the larger output exceed the costs of this government activity—the expenses of operating the commissions and the losses incurred by changing the incentive patterns which then induce distortions in the utilities' cost curves.

2. Fire protection approximates a public good. With the possible exceptions of natural disaster or wholesale arson, fire protection may be jointly consumed by households and businesses in the same area. Exclusion is theoretically possible, but if this is done in an urban area, strong externalities arise because a fire can rapidly spread from one structure to others. In a rural area the externalities of exclusion are lower, but at a minimum it is inconvenient to exclude residents from fire protection.

While the number demanding fire protection in a given area varies substantially, it is rarely lower than fifty. Usually it is much larger. Fire protection is thus a public good demanded by a large group. As discussed in Chapter 13, insufficient amounts of such a good will be provided through the marketplace or through voluntary organizations. An effective way to supply such a good is through collective action, as has occurred in the fire protection area.

The costs of government involvement in fire protection are not insubstantial. Still, the benefits of such involvement far outweigh the costs, since without government intervention in this area much too little fire protection would be provided. The net benefit of this government activity is thus markedly positive.

Another important point arises from the fact that in some areas fire protection is furnished by commercial firms on a contractual basis. This illustrates the principle that because a service is a public good does not necessarily mean that it must be actually produced by a government unit. Returning to Chapter 13, the involvement of the Property Owners' Association resolved the mosquito question, but it was not necessary for the association itself to perform the spraying/drainage procedures. Instead, once the basis for collective action had been established, commercial firms could be employed for these tasks.

3. The deductibility of interest payments decreases their effective price. Consumers are thus encouraged to make purchases which entail interest payments. The largest such purchase for most individuals is a home, which may be a single family dwelling, a duplex, a condominium, or a cooperative apartment. By decreasing interest costs, the tax code increases the demand to buy housing, which in turn reduces the demand to rent housing. Similarly, the tax law raises the demand for automobiles and other durable goods.

From a public interest standpoint, is there a rationale for the tax deductibility of interest payments? The answer is largely no. Capital markets are relatively competitive; no market abnormality exists which makes interest rates systematically too high for consumers. Nor is there evidence which suggests that interest rates do not reflect this country's prevailing preferences for present as opposed to future consumption. Further, the markets for both purchased and rental housing are competitive. Even if they were not, the appropriate government action would not be to make interest payments tax deductible.

This tax provision thus does not have significant benefits from a public interest viewpoint. It does have substantial costs, because it distorts the markets for housing, cars, and other durable goods. For example, the tax law encourages Americans to purchase automobiles at a time when other government departments are trying to discourage car travel. It is therefore likely that the costs of this government intervention clearly exceed its benefits.

217

What then accounts for its widespread acceptance? As is often true, the factor responsible at least in part is distribution effects. This provision is highly beneficial to the middle class, especially those who own single family houses. It is also advantageous to the upper class because the value of a tax deduction rises as income increases. It is disadvantageous to the poor who often do not own houses or other durable goods. Even more important, a tax deduction has only modest value to anyone with a low income. Further, this provision benefits a number of powerful industries. Among them are the construction, lending, and automobile industries.

This case illustrates two important points. First, a factor often responsible for government intervention is not pursuit of the public interest, but rather distribution effects favorable to certain groups. Second, taxes are a powerful regulatory mechanism. They impact almost every American; the tax system is administered by one of the more efficient government agencies, the Internal Revenue Service. Revising the tax code is thus frequently more successful in changing producer or consumer behavior than is direct regulation. While a multitude of government actions have been designed to benefit the housing industry, it is likely that none has been more effective than the tax provision discussed here.

4. Like Skylark's air pollution in Chapter 13, water pollution is a classic example of externalities at work. The polluting entity reaps most of the gains from polluting, but suffers few of the losses. It is therefore led to overpollute, i.e., to discharge more wastes than is optimal from a public interest perspective. Alternatively, as discussed in Chapter 13, pollution can be viewed as a public-good issue or as a common-property problem. In terms of the latter, the use of water as a waste receptacle has either been free or grossly underpriced. Water has therefore been treated as common property, and as a result overused. In terms of the former, water quality is a public good desired by a large group. It is therefore underproduced in the private marketplace.

A hypothetical but representative example of water pollution from a single source is presented in Figure 14–2, which shows the marginal social gain and the marginal social cost of the pollution. Analogous to the decision rule for operating a utility from a welfare-maximizing standpoint, the quantity of water pollution is optimal from a public interest viewpoint when the marginal social gain of pollution equals its marginal social cost. This occurs at Q_0 amount of pollution. To achieve this pollution level, the regulatory agency should charge an effluent fee per unit of pollution equal to F_0. The agency can also achieve this result by adopting a regulation specifying that the pollution level shall not exceed

Figure 14-2

Optimal Level of Pollution

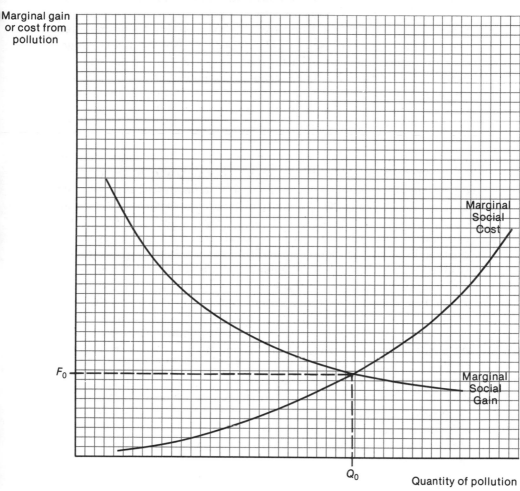

Q_0, relying on the polluter's pursuit of its own interests to increase the quantity of pollution from zero to Q_0.

The difficulty in pollution control lies in estimating the curves presented in Figure 14–2. It is not too hard in this instance to measure marginal social gain since most of the benefits from pollution are garnered by the single polluter. It becomes progressively more difficult to do so as the number of polluters increases. Even more important, estimation of marginal social cost is fraught with problems. Pollution costs fall on many individuals; and some of the costs are highly subjective, e.g., losses experienced by smelling a polluted river.

This is not to say that measurement difficulties cannot be overcome. Useful approximations can frequently be made. Polar cases of egregious pollution can be outlawed. Conversely, discharge of innocuous materials can be sanctioned. Because of their contrasting advantages, a combination of regulations and effluent fees may often prove useful. For example, if one waste treatment technique is modestly less expensive but much less effective than others, it can be banned through regulation. In contrast, if discharge of a pollutant harms water quality but in a moderate and relatively linear manner, an effluent fee is often the appropriate action.

An array of techniques, ranging from complex quantitative analyses to adroit political maneuvers, can thus be employed to increase the effectiveness of pollution control. Even so, it remains true that pollution control faces not only the customary difficulties associated with government regulation, but also the necessity to establish a sound foundation of knowledge on which to base its decisions. This type of regulation thus entails large information costs. To some extent this is true for many kinds of regulation, but it is particularly striking for pollution control.

Purposeful water quality regulation is relatively new in the United States. It is likely that to date its benefits exceed its costs. While the latter are not trivial, the former are probably substantial since prior to this government effort serious overpollution was common in this country. At a minimum the water pollution problem has received widespread publicity. However, water quality control in the United States is not yet an effective ongoing system, certainly not as compared to some parts of Europe, especially the Ruhr region of western Germany. The real test of the government effort to control water pollution will thus come in the future. It may be successful. Or, it may not because of measurement difficulties, government inertia, industry capture, and/or other factors.

5. This FAA function is an example of quality regulation. That is, it is not directed toward reducing the price of the product or toward changing the product's distribution. Rather, the intent of the regulation is to assure the quality of the product.

Any type of quality regulation rests on the premise that for some reason the consumer is not knowledgeable about the product. If the consumer is knowledgeable, quality regulation is redundant. For example, if livestock buyers can judge the quality of cattle, there is no need for a government program certifying cattle. Further, it is not necessary for all consumers to be knowledgeable. Instead, all that is required is for a critical mass to be knowledgeable. Depending upon how differentiated the industry is, that critical mass may be as low as 10 percent or as high as 70 percent of the potential clientele.

Consumers may lack knowledgeability for several reasons. First, the product may be complex and consumers may have insufficient technical expertise to understand it. Second, important product components may be hidden from view after the product is completed. If so, it may be necessary to inspect their quality while work is still in progress. Third, the product may comprise only a tiny fraction of the consumer's total purchases so that it is not worthwhile for him or her to carefully assess its quality.

Commercial airlines are the principal buyers of commercial aircraft. Do one or more of the above reasons apply to them? That is, is there a rationale for suspecting that commercial airlines are uninformed consumers? The answer is no. While airplanes are complex machines, airlines possess sufficient technical expertise to rigorously evaluate them. Aircraft constitute the largest single purchase for airlines. A strong incentive thus exists for carefully assessing aircraft quality, both while work is in progress and after the planes are completed.

Thus, far from being uninformed, airlines are in fact highly knowledgeable customers. Further, this knowledgeability is reinforced by two factors. First, the airline can be sued for large sums if it errs in evaluating the quality of a plane. Second, each flight has a pilot and a crew, who have a strong incentive to monitor the quality and safety of the aircraft.

What then is the benefit of this FAA function? It can be argued that since aircraft safety is extremely important, any gain in safety is worth the cost. At the extreme this argument becomes untenable since it would justify large expenditures for imperceptible gains. Even accepting this argument to some extent, it remains uncertain that the benefits of this FAA function exceed its costs.

Further, it appears that at times a close alliance has existed between the FAA and aircraft manufacturers. This suggests that the latter may have partially captured the former. This development is not surprising since aircraft manufacturers constitute a small group which has large interests at stake. Nor does partial capture necessarily undermine the FAA's effectiveness as an independent voice. However, since partial capture often reduces regulatory effectiveness, the apparent alliance existing at times between the FAA and aircraft manufacturers casts additional doubt on the net benefit of the former's regulation of airplane quality.

Index